The Catholic Reformation: A Very Short Introduction

VERY SHORT INTRODUCTIONS are for anyone wanting a stimulating and accessible way into a new subject. They are written by experts, and have been translated into more than 45 different languages.

The series began in 1995, and now covers a wide variety of topics in every discipline. The VSI library currently contains over 750 volumes—a Very Short Introduction to everything from Psychology and Philosophy of Science to American History and Relativity—and continues to grow in every subject area.

Very Short Introductions available now:

For more information visit our website

www.oup.com/vsi/

James E. Kelly

THE CATHOLIC REFORMATION

A Very Short Introduction

OXFORD
UNIVERSITY PRESS

Great Clarendon Street, Oxford, OX2 6DP,
United Kingdom

Oxford University Press is a department of the University of Oxford.
It furthers the University's objective of excellence in research, scholarship,
and education by publishing worldwide. Oxford is a registered trade mark of
Oxford University Press in the UK and in certain other countries

Published in the United States of America by Oxford University Press
198 Madison Avenue, New York, NY 10016, United States of America

British Library Cataloguing in Publication Data

Data available

Library of Congress Control Number: 2024942420

ISBN 9780192862310

Printed and bound by
CPI Group (UK) Ltd, Croydon, CR0 4YY

Links to third party websites are provided by Oxford in good faith and
for information only. Oxford disclaims any responsibility for the materials
contained in any third party website referenced in this work.

The manufacturer's authorised representative in the EU for product safety is Oxford
University Press España S.A. of El Parque Empresarial San Fernando de Henares, Avenida
de Castilla, 2 – 28830 Madrid (www.oup. es/en or product.safety@oup.com). OUP España
S.A. also acts as importer into Spain of products made by the manufacturer.

Contents

List of illustrations

Chapter 1
Defining a new movement

In the south-east of England in the early 1590s, a Jesuit named John Gerard squeezed himself into a small, secret hiding space under a fireplace. The house stood in open countryside, meaning the family sheltering him had been able to spot the early morning raiding party as it surrounded the building. An informant had provided intelligence that Gerard was somewhere in the house; if caught, he would be charged as a traitor for his Catholic priesthood and hanged, drawn, and quartered, while those who sheltered him could be charged as felons and face the noose. Gerard had been living with the family and covertly ministering in the area for a few years. In that time, he had sought to bring about a total spiritual reformation of the household, reorientating it towards God through the introduction of a near-monastic model of life. He weaned the family off their commitment to traditional, medieval fasting habits, which apart from being outdated, was also dangerous behaviour in an officially Protestant country.

In place of these external expressions of faith, Gerard encouraged internal spiritual commitment to Catholicism, with specific adaptations for the situation in Protestant England; Gerard himself publicly disguised his priesthood by dressing as a gentleman, riding a horse, and joining card games as part of his missionary activity. This covert approach to ministry even raised eyebrows among those who secretly adhered to Catholicism.

Gerard had originally arrived in the house to displace the former family chaplain, a priest who had been ordained during the reign of the Catholic Mary I more than 30 years earlier. According to Gerard, this chaplain was constantly at odds with the younger clergy who had been arriving from mainland Europe since the 1570s. Indeed, he found the Jesuit particularly irritating, decrying him as a 'meddlesome innovator', seemingly shocked by Gerard's 'new' European-learnt ways. Yet here Gerard was, a man born in England but educated on the Continent and ordained in Rome, hiding in a cramped, dark space under a bedroom fireplace, while his compatriots tore apart the house in their manhunt.

Gerard would survive the search undiscovered, though debilitated by the days spent in the hiding space with no food or drink. He would later be caught at another location; after imprisonment and torture at the Tower of London he famously escaped via something akin to a zipline running from one tower down to the edge of the River Thames. With the situation too perilous in England, he was smuggled out of the country and spent the rest of his life training priests to return undercover to the homeland he himself would never again see.

In this short account of John Gerard's action-packed life can be found a number of the key themes of the Catholic Reformation: the centrality of personal spiritual reform, missionary activity, persecution and martyrdom, adaptation to specific national situations, the relationship between national and international movements, and the idea that, even within the Catholic world, something had changed. Indeed, in his suspicion of these new-fangled Catholic ideas coming from the Continent, the older Catholic priest was not merely an isolated, cantankerous elder. Living in a land officially cut off from the opening salvo of the Catholic Reformation, these older clergy had not encountered the new, Tridentine Catholicism, which deemed them, according to William Allen, the leader of the English mission, 'insufficiently instructed for the necessities of the present time in all the duties of religion and the Church's censures', and needing 'more appropriate instruction'. Something had been stirring on the Continent and the faith those older men thought they knew had changed: the Catholic Reformation had been unleashed.

The importance of a name

Certain historiographical judgements have already been implied in the above few paragraphs. What to call this movement and how to define the timespan involved are questions of continuing debate among historians, further complicated by the fact that the two are inextricably linked. Certainly, in the English-speaking world and, to a degree, other European nations, the movement has frequently been referred to as the Counter-Reformation, a name that carries its own baggage and assumptions, particularly in those countries that have a historical Protestant identity.

The term 'Counter-Reformation' has its roots in Germany in the late 18th century. It was used to describe events in the Holy Roman Empire that saw the return to Catholicism—sometimes by force—of those regions that had dallied with Protestantism between roughly 1555 and the Treaty of Westphalia in 1648 that ended the Thirty Years War. In other words, it was used to describe the re-Catholicization of areas, the recovery of lands to a majority—whether enforced or not—Catholic population.

The term 'Counter-Reformation' grew in popularity during the 19th century and began to be used more broadly, applied not only to developments in the geographical territories of the Holy Roman Empire but also the whole of Europe and judged to be the Catholic Church's response to the Protestant reformations of the 16th century. In this historical interpretation, the Counter-Reformation had been born after the Catholic Church was shocked into belated action by the breakaway of Protestantism, awakening with horror from its arrogant stupor. Although something of a caricature of the historical interpretation, one can easily appreciate how it took root in countries that had identified as Protestant since the early modern period. Implied in the term 'Counter-Reformation' were assumptions of a Catholic passivity that morphed into a reactionary, backward-looking counter-attack, its start date pinpointed to the calling of the Council of Trent as a belated response to Martin Luther's actions two decades earlier. As such, this historiographical viewpoint was Euro-centric; it prioritized Catholic recovery of lands from Protestantism and defined its start and cut-off dates according to European events, neglecting the global aspect of the movement.

Although it might still include the loaded word 'reformation', this movement will be referred to as the Catholic Reformation throughout this book. Other terms could be applied, such as the period of Catholic reform or Catholic renewal, which convey something of what was happening but do not, perhaps, impress just how far-reaching it was. Naming it the Catholic Reformation is an attempt to underline that this was an active, creative movement, adapted to new spiritual and material realities, emphasizing that it was a modernizing movement rather than one simply looking to turn back the clock, or at least keep it stuck at the same time.

Another element worth considering was identified by French historians in the 20th century and that is the Catholic Reformation as an attempt at Christianization. Such an interpretation may go too far—implying as it does that the preceding centuries were virtually pagan—but toned down, it makes a lot of sense to view the Catholic Reformation also as a belt-tightening exercise. There was a recognition that some elements of Christianity had got out of hand, whether that be local saint cults or the more infamous end of the indulgence business. To address this, key aims of the Catholic reform movement were better trained clergy, catechesis, evangelization, and battling superstition.

If the Catholic Reformation is understood in that light, then it becomes what might be termed a (very) long reformation and, from the Church's perspective, actually its entire purpose. The Catholic Reformation had deep foundations and was not an unprecedented explosion; indeed, Catholicism had been here before, such as with the Gregorian reforms of the 11th century or the burst of reform in the 13th century that itself involved a council (the Fourth Lateran one of 1215) and famously saw the emergence of new religious orders, such as the Dominicans and, notably, the Franciscans, as Francis of Assisi heard the call to rebuild the Church. In other words, Catholicism had faced challenges of internal stagnation and external assault before. It also had experience of recognizing the need to reform itself, and there was an established path to achieving this, reforming councils having previously sought to distil orthodoxy for the laity.

Having established its long origins, it is also worth displacing the date older schools of history judged the Catholic Reformation's end point. Though the Treaty of Westphalia in 1648 may make sense in political interpretations of the period and if one only thinks of a very European-centred Counter-Reformation, it fails to acknowledge that the Catholic Reformation happened at different times in different places around the globe. Indeed, proponents of the Catholic Enlightenment in the 18th century viewed themselves as best serving the needs—and implementing the central tenets—of the Catholic Reformation. In the 19th century, in areas on the peripheries of the traditional heartlands of the Catholic Reformation, one can find church figures self-consciously implementing the decrees of the Council of Trent. This was a long, even continual, Catholic Reformation.

Tracking the Catholic Reformation

The Protestant Reformation and its legacy is without doubt a pivotal moment in history. But in terms of movements that went global and affected the most people, the Catholic Reformation is arguably *the* event in the early modern period, playing at least as significant a role in shaping the world today. Rather than being simply oppressive and obsessively homogenizing, it unleashed bursts of creativity that changed the spiritual and, indeed, sensory experience of everywhere it touched. While on the one hand it offered a universality of experience, differences in interpretation and implementation as it adapted to cultural circumstance, particularly at its greatest geographical extent, created a two-way relationship between the Catholic world's traditional centres and its new peripheries. Due to its geographic breadth and scope of vision, it is almost impossible to write a full, comprehensive overview of the Catholic Reformation, a task made even more complicated by lack of consensus about the time period involved. This book makes no claim to do that. Instead, it presents an overview of the Catholic Reformation, suggesting ways of understanding it, highlighting thematic threads that run through the chapters to offer a concise introduction to a global movement. The book features the expected, such as spiritual and religious matters, and how they entwined with the political, but also covers the full gamut of experience of the Catholic Reformation, including its deliberately sensory approach in terms of art, architecture, and music. As well as introducing the reader to the breadth of the Catholic Reformation experience in concise form, the book sets it within recent historiographical debates, thus presenting a provocative discussion of the topic's central issues.

Within these pages, the Catholic Reformation is tracked from its beginnings in the first half of the 16th century—pre-dating the Council of Trent, which is frequently viewed as its starting point—through the years of unrest in Europe, to its global expansion in the Americas, Asia, and Africa, and its continued influence and legacy into the 20th century. The second chapter opens by exploring the long roots of the Catholic Reformation in the growing recognition from the end of the 15th century that the Church was in need of renewal. It includes the reform of religious orders and the creation of new ones, with two of the most important—the Jesuits and the Capuchins—coming into existence before the Council of Trent. As such, the chapter argues that the Council did not simply pronounce against Protestant teachings, but defined orthodoxy and gave official expression to some of the earlier Catholic reformers' plans. One element in particular was the model Catholic Reformation bishop, as embodied by Charles Borromeo. The chapter finishes by touching upon a common theme that runs throughout the book: that what happened after Trent—that is, the Catholic Reformation—involved a burst of creativity which often had little or nothing to do with what was pronounced at the council. This meant that there were different visions of how to achieve Catholic Reformation, and divergent approaches could rub up against each other, even when both were considered completely orthodox.

The following two chapters give an overview of the geographical extent of the Catholic Reformation. Chapter 3 focuses on Catholic Europe, starting with the traditional heartlands of the movement: Spain, Portugal, and the Italian states. Although there was genuine spiritual renewal in all these regions, Catholicism in Spain and Portugal was particularly idiosyncratic, believing its nationally bonded vision to be the true way of expressing the faith, a view that was to have significant global repercussions. The second geographic cluster considers those European nations of more contested reformations. In these arenas, the Catholic Reformation can be viewed as successfully pushing back against a wave of Protestant defections, through different methods of co-opting or working alongside secular powers to achieve these recoveries. From the great success of Catholic reform in the Low Countries and to a lesser degree the Polish–Lithuanian Commonwealth, to the rebuilding—both figuratively and literally—of Catholicism in France and the German states after the ravages of religious wars, to the failures in the Balkan regions, the chapter shows the Catholic Reformation being implemented at different times and in different ways across the various nations. Chapter 4 sees this phenomenon played out on the world stage through missionary work. The global mission had two targets: areas previously untouched by the Christian gospel, and those places 'lost' to Protestantism. The chapter opens with the Iberian missions in the Americas; pre-dating the Council of Trent, missionary activity here was yoked to colonialist expansion, an Iberian understanding of Catholicism very much welding it to forced Europeanization. However, there were Catholic reformers strongly opposed to this approach, leading to creative adaptations that often ran counter to the official Iberian position on how missionaries should go about their work. The prioritization of colonialism also predominated in the parts of Africa under Iberian control, but a very different approach to missionary activity was evident in the Asian arena. In the missions to India, China, and Japan, working independently from secular colonial interests, methods of accommodation and inculturation flourished. Unlike endeavours to spread the gospel to the furthest corners of the world, the Dutch Republic and England saw missions to a persecuted Catholic community, particularly the martyrs of the latter. Paired with activity in the Asian arena, these global missionary efforts gripped the imagination of Catholic Europe and helped shape it, underlining the reciprocal circles of influence between centres and peripheries in the Catholic Reformation.

Chapters 5 and 6 shift focus to look at what it meant to be Catholic in this era of reform. Chapter 5 opens by considering sanctity and the new type of exemplary life raised up by the Church for imitation, drawing from figures across its newly global purview. At the heart of the Catholic Reformation was an effort to provoke genuine spiritual reform and commitment in every individual, and the site of most of these efforts was the parish church, with initiatives to improve preaching and catechesis, emphasize the sacramental cycle, and promote the devotional life. The chapter ends by considering the innovative approaches taken not just in these initiatives, but also in theology more broadly. Unsurprisingly, this creativity also provoked flashpoints around conflicting theological interpretations and viewpoints. This resulted in push back by other supposed engines of Catholic reform, in particular the Iberian-specific Inquisition and the Index of banned books.

These tensions explain why so many now viewed as standard bearers of the Catholic Reformation, such as Teresa of Avila, the Capuchins, and even Ignatius of Loyola and the Jesuit way of life, ran into trouble with those who considered themselves the real holders of Tridentine orthodoxy. The chapter shows, again, not just the overarching pastoral intent of the Catholic Reformation, but also how different it looked across the globe. Chapter 6 picks up these threads to show the sheer breadth of Catholic Reformation ambition. Affecting the whole sensory gamut, the chapter details how art, architecture, drama, and the intellectual world were embraced by an all-encompassing Catholic reform agenda that aimed to inspire genuine spiritual renewal in every individual.

The final chapter concentrates on the legacies of the Catholic Reformation. It further elaborates on the competing interpretations of what Catholic reform should look like by detailing several major disagreements, strands of which offered different paths down which the Catholic Reformation could have ventured before their official repudiation. The chapter argues that the movement is best understood as a long Catholic Reformation, pushing at the boundaries of previous methods of evangelization right through to the late 18th century's Catholic Enlightenment before a centralizing, ultra-papalist approach kicked in in the 19th century. Nevertheless, threads of the Catholic Reformation were still evident in the second half of the 20th century at the international church council known as Vatican II, in terms both of intent and method, but also witnessed in the council having to grapple with issues that were never settled satisfactorily throughout the whole Catholic Reformation period. There can be a popular perception that those in the modern period are the first to have to think in terms of the entire planet; this book underlines that the Catholic Reformation was one of the first worldwide movements and saw Catholicism become the first global religion.

Chapter 2
The Council of Trent and new soldiers for Christ

One view of the Council of Trent is that it was a knee-jerk reaction to the progressive ideas of the Protestant reformers, albeit a paradoxically belated one indicative of the dysfunction of the Catholic Church from which the modernizers were breaking free. Regardless of how inappropriate it is to apply modern concepts such as progressive and conservative to the early modern world, this understanding has a limited basis in reality. The Council of Trent was as much a belt-tightening exercise within Catholicism—that had, in fact, been a long time coming—as it was an effort to maintain business as usual. The Protestant Reformation may have provided the short-term impetus for the council, shocking complacent elements within the Church to finally listen to the calls of reformers, but the need for renewal had been recognized decades earlier. The Council of Trent and, more accurately, the Catholic Reformation, can best be understood as part of the continual waxing and waning of the Church through the previous centuries, with parallels to previous bouts of reform, such as the boom in mendicant orders in the 13th century that helped revive the Church.

In short, the Catholic Reformation had its roots in medieval efforts at religious renewal and, to a degree, the Council of Trent can be viewed as part of an ongoing process from late medieval Catholic reform. Vital to these developments was the conciliar movement of the 15th century. Faced with the papal schism, which saw three competing claimants to the papacy, plus the rise of the Hussites in Bohemia, the Holy Roman Emperor Sigismund had called the Council of Constance in 1414. Apart from condemning the Hussite leader, Jan Hus, as a heretic, the council concluded, importantly, that papal authority was subject to canon law. Therefore, a canonically constituted collective body—such as a church council—could make authoritative decisions. Thus, from what appears to be a very dry piece of bureaucracy, the seeds of the Catholic Reformation, that would be kick-started by the 16th-century Council of Trent, were sown. Moreover, the Council of Constance showed the important role a layperson, in this case the Holy Roman Emperor, could play in compelling the Church to reform itself.

Attempts at renewal and reinvigoration were also happening away from headline-grabbing church councils. Socially active lay movements and confraternities were increasing in number, with many focused on the centrality of the eucharist. Criticism of absentee bishops was on the rise; in response, a new model was offered by Giovanni Matteo Giberti (1495–1543), bishop of Verona. Encouraging clergy and laity to work side by side in charitable initiatives, Giberti also created a designated diocesan seminary to train an educated clergy, as well as initiating programmes for the religious instruction of both adults and children. Other notable figures were talking in similar ways that could easily have come from more famous Catholic Reformation figures; the fifth Lateran Council, held between 1512 and 1517, though something of a failure in its attempt to quell unrest within the Church, heard from the Augustinian Giles of Viterbo at the opening session, 'Men must be transformed by religion, not religion by men', the very language of internal spiritual reform.

A particularly strong impulse for reform was growing in the Iberian peninsula, led by the monastic and mendicant orders, which enjoyed episcopal support and had full royal backing. This

union of state and Church had been solidified at the Council of
Seville in 1478, when the crown and the bishops had agreed they
would seek reform of the Church together rather than wait for—or
risk—outside interference. This binding of the secular and the
spiritual would become a marker of the Catholic Reformation in
Iberian spheres of influence. It meant Spain had an episcopate
used to and desirous of reform, who would go on to be influential at
the Council of Trent. Equally, the observant religious orders were
at the forefront of these reform efforts in the opening decades of
the 16th century. For example, the Benedictine Congregation of
Valladolid was a movement committed to strict observance of
the order's rule, monks often travelling to reform other houses,
while prizing high-quality preaching. Garcia de Cisneros, a
spiritual leader within the congregation, was sent to reform the
Benedictine monastery at Montserrat, where he composed his
Exercitatorio de la vida espiritual (*Exercises for the Spiritual Life*,
1500), a guide to personal, interior spiritual contemplation. It is
thus unsurprising that the most famous reform order, the Society
of Jesus, emerged from this Iberian environment, its founder
Ignatius of Loyola having been given a copy of Cisneros's book
during his pivotal stay at the Montserrat monastery in 1522.

Religious orders—reforming the old and creating the new, part 1

Reform movements had a long history within religious orders, both
male and female, but there was a significant increase in such
initiatives in the decades leading up to the era of Reformation,
a trajectory that was given new impetus by the Catholic
Reformation. Not for nothing had Martin Luther, the figurehead
of the Protestant Reformation, been a member of the observant
Augustinians. The observant branches of various mendicant orders
had been gaining traction since the 14th century and began to
wield significant influence within their respective orders during
the first half of the 15th century. They sought a more active,
committed following of their original rule and life by advocating

better theological training and formation of novices. As well as the Augustinians, the Carmelites and Dominicans boasted similar observant movements and their influence as the Catholic Reformation gained pace cannot be underestimated. For example, the Dominicans went on to staff the Inquisition and maintain the Index of banned books, styling themselves as defenders of Catholic orthodoxy.

Reform within the Franciscans was more complex. By 1517, efforts to finally bring to a close a centuries-old debate about how best to live Franciscan poverty had resulted in the official separation of the two traditions, the Conventuals and the Observants. Other branches developed as the momentum of the Catholic Reformation grew, but arguably the most significant grouping to appear in the reformed Franciscan style were the Capuchins. Judging their community's observance of Franciscan ideals as too lax, several ascetical friars, including Matteo de Bascio, broke away to live according to what they viewed as the original austerity of St Francis of Assisi. In 1528 they received papal approval for their way of life and, despite opposition, by 1535 there were 35 houses of the Capuchins and around 700 friars. In 1536, Bernardino d'Asti gave the breakaways real shape and devoted them to the care of souls and preaching, prompting some of the original adherents to leave.

The new movement was almost dealt a fatal blow when its newly elected fourth general, Bernardino Ochino, was accused of holding Lutheran sympathies and fled to Geneva and Protestantism in 1542. This led to the Capuchins being officially confined to Italy, but this restriction was soon relaxed, and by 1587 they had expanded to around 6,000 members, which would rise to nearly 30,000 in the 17th century. Donning rough habits with distinctive hoods, they dedicated themselves to creating a better-educated and more committed Catholic laity. Preaching in plain language to the poor during travelling parish missions, they also cared for the sick and fed the hungry, gaining immense popularity, especially for their dedication during outbreaks of plague. Patronized by lay and clerical elites, the Capuchins became beacons of charity in Italy and Catholic Reformation fighters elsewhere, their importance to the movement unfairly neglected in modern historians' over-focus on the Jesuits.

As well as redirecting the old, new ways of doing things were being found. Several of the most significant pioneers of Catholic renewal had direct experience of war and the military. Gaetano di Thiene, better known now as Cajetan, was tortured by Spanish soldiers during the Sack of Rome in 1527 but, by that time, along with Gian Pietro Carafa, he had already received approval for a new congregation, the Theatines, from *Thiate*, the Latin for Chieti, where Carafa had been bishop. Aimed at the spiritual renewal and reform of the clergy, the group emphasized priestly duties, such as preaching, praying the Office (daily prayers expected to be said by a priest), pastoral activity, and worthy celebration of the Mass. From unsteady beginnings, the Theatines blossomed when Carafa was elected Pope Paul IV in 1555. Called to reform the breviary, the Theatines became crucial as a source of new, active bishops, characterized by residence in their dioceses and advocates of reform through doctrinal orthodoxy, thus embodying the Tridentine ideal. Though they did not flourish outside Italy, the Theatines would go on to be present in the arenas of global reform, such as Sumatra and Borneo. In practice, they represented a middle ground between the traditional monastic orders—through communal recitation of the Office and commitment to an austere life—and a newer model of activism.

Elsewhere in Italy, the medical studies graduate and priest Antonio Maria Zaccaria established with others the Clerics Regular of St Paul in Milan. More popularly known as the Barnabites after taking over a church dedicated to that saint, they were focused on missions to the people and devotion to the eucharist through initiatives such as the *Quarant'Ore*, which involved 40 hours of prayer before a displayed consecrated host. An ascetic and reforming movement, they worked alongside a group of lay women, the Angelicals of St Paul, founded by Luisa Torelli in 1530. The Barnabites were approved in 1579 after their life was examined by a leading architect of the Catholic Reformation, Charles Borromeo; he frequently took retreats at their house in Milan and one of their number went on to act as his confessor.

Borromeo also invited to his diocese the Clerks Regular of Somascha. Founded by the then-layman Girolamo Emiliani in Venice, the group was briefly merged with the Theatines in the middle of the 16th century. Granted papal confirmation in 1568, they were dedicated to the care and education of orphans and poor youth. Notably, the above three movements all relied upon patronage from the nobility and sought to minister to the ills around them, both social and ecclesiastical. Northern and central Italy at that time was continuously afflicted by conflict, and Cajetan was not the only reformer to have direct experience of it; Emiliani had been a prisoner of war, before experiencing religious conversion.

Perhaps the most famous of the era's new orders also owed its existence to war. Hailing from a noble family in the Basque region of Spain, the man who would come to be known as Ignatius of Loyola was an officer in the service of the governor of Navarre. Ignatius's legs were badly injured by a cannonball during the French force's siege of Pamplona in 1521, resulting in a lengthy convalescence. This period witnessed his gradual spiritual awakening, from default cultural Catholicism to full spiritual engagement. Having slowly gathered a group of companions around him, Ignatius set about securing formal recognition for a new order, which was confirmed by Pope Paul III in the tellingly titled papal bull *Regimini Militantis Ecclesiae* ('To the Government of the Church Militant'). Known as the Society of Jesus, or the Jesuits, the order boasted a number of novelties. Unlike previous groups, it observed no communal liturgical life of set prayers in a chapel, nor a set rota of fasting, plus the time till final profession of lifetime vows was far lengthier than the norm. In addition to the traditional vows of poverty, chastity, and obedience, the Jesuits added a fourth vow of obedience to the pope. This vow partly explains their exemption from episcopal authority; they could preach and administer the sacraments where they wanted without needing the permission of the local bishop. Moreover, a firm line of authority ran right through the new order: strongly centralized along military lines of command to inculcate unity, the order was led by a superior general whose decision was final on all matters, and was elected for life. All these factors combined to mean that there was opposition to the Jesuits from the start; they did not look or behave like a traditional religious order, were suspected of being a tool of papal supremacy, and were accused of breathtaking arrogance in their choice of name.

In many ways, the opponents of the Jesuits were right; they were something of a revolution, but one that would be hugely successful. Loosely dedicated to preaching, teaching, and acts of caritas, the two former aims would come to dominate due to the circumstances of the time. Preaching and mission will be dealt with in later chapters, but teaching came to hold a central place in the new Society, as they educated what would become a new lay and clerical elite. By 1551 the Roman College had been founded and the order was receiving invitations to open educational establishments all over Europe.

The growth was remarkable: by the mid-18th century, the Society numbered over 25,000 members staffing more than 800 educational institutions across the globe. Yet for all their novelty, there was something resolutely old-fashioned about the Jesuits. They quickly shifted their focus to education because they recognized the need for real spiritual formation. Their ideas about obedience were motivated not, at least notionally, by slavish papalism, but obedience to God. They were driven by the need for inner spiritual renewal, an evangelical work that had been the clarion call for pastoral reform within the Church over the centuries. Despite a number of structures that appear specifically designed to counter Protestant assault, it is notable that the Jesuits were founded with little mention of anti-Protestant activity. That is not to say they did not bolster Catholicism: Diego Lainez and Alfonso Salmerón, both original companions of Ignatius, served as papal theologians during the early sessions of the Council of Trent. Ultimately, the Jesuits' motivation was spiritual reformation as they combined the more traditional contemplative approach with a vigorous dedication to action.

Council of Trent

Millions of words have been written on the Council of Trent's labyrinthine travails but the important developments of early modern Catholicism were not so much about what happened at the various sessions, but what came after. What might be termed the spirit of the Council of Trent motivated much of what is associated with the Catholic Reformation, despite a good deal of it not being mentioned or only featuring fleetingly in the documents promulgated by the council. Nevertheless, when the council finally met, it was faced with a number of questions, the most important being its aim: was it to deal with religious schism, or to give an official launchpad to the reform movements mentioned above?

The trigger for an official programme of internal Catholic renewal was the defections from the Church spurred by Europe's Protestant Reformations. Traditional historiography once placed prime emphasis on this context, which undoubtedly shocked influential voices into calling for the council. Luther's movement had gained such traction that, by 1545, only Bavaria really remained a Catholic stronghold in central Europe. The Protestant princes of the Holy Roman Empire had joined together in the Schmalkaldic League and were bound to defend the movement against both papacy and emperor, underlining another binary:

secular and ecclesiastical authority. Protestantism's influence was spreading, with new movements emerging in places such as France and the Polish–Lithuanian Commonwealth, while England was already into its own version of Reformation. The emperor, Charles V, was growing increasingly desperate, unsure of how to deal with the twin pressures of burgeoning Protestantism in his own lands and the threat of the Ottoman Turks to the south. At the same time, Pope Paul III was wary of challenges to papal authority and viewed the Protestant movement as just another in a long line of heresies that the Church had dealt with over the centuries. Paul III nonetheless represented the bridge between the older style Renaissance pope interested in secular glory and a new breed who recognized the need for spiritual reform of the Church. He had already reorganized the Roman Inquisition with Carafa at the forefront, plus had commissioned a group of cardinals, including Carafa and England's Reginald Pole, to draw up a report on the state of the Church. They were openly critical of bishops not residing in their dioceses, abuse of indulgences, the quasi-secular lifestyle of the Roman curia, and even the role of the pope himself.

After several false starts, the council eventually opened at Trent on 13 December 1545 (Figure 1). The location was a compromise as it lay in the lands of the Holy Roman Empire but on the Italian side of the Alps. The council would go on to run, intermittently, for 18 years; this first session lasted only till 1549 and included a controversial move to Bologna, a site more conducive to papal influence. Despite being invited, the German Protestants refused to attend the session, prompting Charles V to start a war against them. Relationships were similarly tense within the council and gradually broke down over procedures and differences between, for want of better terms, papalist and reformist visions. Still, several key dogmatic issues were decided. Unlike Protestant prioritization of scripture, the Council decreed that there were two sources of divine revelation: scripture and tradition. Another key moment was the council's support for the Latin

1. Engraving of the Council of Trent in session (16th century).

Vulgate version of the Bible, though they did recognize that the text needed correcting.

Following Paul III's death in 1550, Giovanni Maria Ciocchi del Monte, who had been cardinal-president at the council's first session, was elected as Julius III. Viewed as a compromise candidate, he recognized the need to recall the council, but was nevertheless wary of Charles V, whom he suspected of wanting reform simply to appease the Protestants in his lands, which could lead to doctrinal compromises. Nevertheless, it was this second meeting of the council, which ran from 1551 to 1552, that witnessed the definitive break with Protestantism. Although Protestant representatives did attend this time, any hopes at reconciliation were ended by the council defining transubstantiation: that at the moment of consecration during the Mass, the wafer and wine became literally the body and blood of Christ, which was anathema to Protestants. Attempts at keeping Protestants within the tent were over. Threat of war led to the early curtailment of the council's sitting while, by 1555, the emperor had signed the Diet of Augsburg, recognizing the Lutheran confession in the Holy Roman Empire.

In the meantime, the reform party within Rome gained the upper hand when Carafa was elected Pope Paul IV in 1555. However, their hopes were quickly dashed when his vision of reform under strict papal leadership, coupled with an anti-Habsburg passion—possibly influenced by what he considered the sell-out of the Diet of Augsburg—ushered in a period of repression. As pope, Carafa dedicated himself to hunting heresy and bolstering the Roman Inquisition; even old reformist colleagues such as Pole were investigated for heresy. A harsh Index of forbidden books was drawn up that included all the works of the humanist reformer Erasmus, and Roman Jews were consigned to a ghetto. When Carafa died, the Roman Inquisition's offices were burnt to the ground by a mob.

Giovanni Angelo Medici had left the curia in 1558 in protest at Paul IV's behaviour; it was him the conclave turned to next, electing him as Pope Pius IV in 1559, and one of his first acts was to pardon the rioting arsonists. It must have seemed to him that things had deteriorated: England had broken with Rome (under Elizabeth I), and in France Jean Calvin inspired the rise of the Huguenots. This gave the new pope all the impetus he needed to recall the council. This time, the German Protestant princes rejected the invitation, but the council already had enough to deal with in balancing the interests of Spain, France, the papacy, and the Holy Roman Empire. The council reconvened in January 1562 and was well attended, including the ambassadors of states such as Portugal, Bavaria, and Florence. Nevertheless, factionalism was rampant. Suspicions this time rose against the French, who attended for the first time but some believed only wanted reforms in an effort to keep the Calvinists inside the national tent. Some sessions descended into mud-slinging; to cap it all, in March 1563, the emperor wrote to the pope effectively saying that Rome could not be trusted to reform itself.

It was not until spring 1563 that things improved with the appointment of Giovanni Morone as cardinal-president of the council. Having previously languished in jail under suspicion of heresy by Carafa, it was Morone who broke the deadlock and secured the most important reforms of Trent. The first of these was to secure agreement on an issue that had rumbled on through every stage of the council: the non-residence of bishops in their dioceses. It was finally agreed that by 'divine command' a bishop should reside in his see. Moreover, the council laid out the responsibilities of a bishop: he should regularly visit the parishes in his diocese and preach frequently, becoming a pastor to his people rather than a distant ruler. The other major issue the Morone-guided council addressed was the poor education and formation of clergy, a matter many saw as a major cause of the Protestant breakaway. Seminaries were to be created in every diocese to form a committed clergy with whom people would have direct contact. Here was the spiritual reform envisioned by the pre-Trent reformers given institutional expression.

Reacting to news that Pius IV was dying, the council issued a flurry of decrees on a number of other matters before closing in December 1563. Yet perhaps more instructive is to consider what was not pronounced upon. Despite the Holy Roman Emperor's ambassador asking about communion under both kinds—that is, for the laity to receive the chalice as well as the host (consecrated wine and bread)—the council left it to the papacy to decide, and sometimes concessions were made. Secular representatives at the council were keen to keep Church–state relationships off the agenda, so these were left aside. The council participants also never touched on the role of the papacy in the Church and its relationship to bishops, a thorny issue that would be stored up for later centuries. Nevertheless, the council had at least partially delivered. The numbers attending were limited, but it was never the case that all bishops were expected to attend. In the form of secular rulers' representatives, the laity helped set the course and, arguably, even drove some of the reform. In its doctrinal decrees, the council had shored up the theological borders of Catholicism, clarifying contentious matters and thus ensuring Catholic confessionalization. Moreover, by securing reform of the bishop's role and the formation of the clergy, the reformist agenda was given impetus, with the pastoral imperative at the fore. Reform would come more slowly to the Roman curia, but it is telling that four of the seven popes elected in the remainder of the 16th century had taken part in the council.

Bishop as reformer

Reform movements had been building before Trent, and its closure did not stop the trend. Reform of secular clergy—that is, priests who did not belong to a religious order—had been pushed through in the latter stages of the council. One of its main advocates seemed an unlikely candidate to champion reform: Charles Borromeo, nephew of Pius IV and a creature of the Roman curia. Borromeo had directed the papal secretariat during the third and final period of the Council of Trent. In that role, he composed most of the dispatches sent on behalf of the pope from Rome regarding the council. Coming soon after some notoriously nepotistic renaissance pontificates, Borromeo's background gave no hint as to the ascetic reformer and model Tridentine bishop he would become (following a personal spiritual reformation prompted by the death of his brother).

Appointed archbishop of Milan in 1564, Borromeo set about implementing the Tridentine reforms in a diocese that had suffered from absentee bishops and spiritual drift; indeed, he was the first archbishop to actually reside there for 80 years. A major part of his work was reviving the social dignity and spiritual credibility of the role of the bishop. He believed that dioceses led by bishops were the foundation stones of the Church, since it was through parish churches that most Catholics experienced the Church and maintained contact with it. Just like the Jesuits and other religious orders, Borromeo emphasized the importance of deep personal spiritual commitment.

The Borromean vision of Catholic reform had many different aspects. Three seminaries were founded for the better training of clergy, one for the city of Milan, one for those destined to work in rural parishes, and another for missionary work in Switzerland. He even formed an elite community of priests to champion reform in the region, the Oblates of St Ambrose, all the while advocating better-trained clergy and a spiritually engaged laity through improved catechesis and regular confession. Other initiatives ranged from regular preaching to church architecture. Importantly, Borromeo harnessed the printing press to develop a blueprint of reform that could be rolled out elsewhere in his *Acta Ecclesiae Mediolanensis* (*Acts of the Church of Milan*). For all that he may appear to have reaffirmed the Church's hierarchical structure, Borromeo was no unthinking papalist. Even *his* approach to reform was questioned, those in Rome making attempts to cool his ardour and rigour, wary of Borromeo's insistence on a bishop's rights within his own diocese. In Borromeo's view, the bishop was in charge in his diocese and he should resist both secular and Roman interference; they were there to support him, not dictate to him. Borromeo's vision was just one interpretation of Trent, drawing on the spirit of reform that pre-dated its convening to give new significance to the role of the bishop in the Tridentine Church.

Unsurprisingly, this vision clashed with that of others, underlining that the Catholic Reformation was not simply a single bloc of opinion. There were different ways of interpreting Tridentine Catholicism and debates became more heated after the council's end. Indeed, Borromeo himself survived an assassination attempt in 1569; Pius V had commissioned him to investigate the Humiliati Order, who were resistant to reform and a symbol of all that had gone wrong in some religious communities, resulting in a friar from the order shooting at him during Mass. Within two years, the order was suppressed and ceased to exist. A less extreme example, but one that shows the clash of Catholic Reformation visions, is Borromeo's relationship with the Jesuits. Maybe wary of what he considered their extreme papalism, Borromeo was uneasy with Jesuit claims of exemption from ordinary ecclesiastical structures and authority. Despite inviting them to his diocese, the relationship gradually worsened before reaching crisis during an outbreak of plague, a period that would conversely cement Borromeo's own Tridentine reputation. As pestilence raged through the city in 1576–7, Borromeo was exasperated by what he perceived as the Jesuits' timidity in caring for the sick. The Jesuits insisted they could not act without the permission of their provincial and the general in Rome, prompting Borromeo to fire back that he was not subject to Jesuit superiors. Moreover, he viewed Jesuit methods, embodied by this refusal, as potentially damaging to ecclesiastical discipline. Thus, to get around what he considered Jesuit intransigence, Borromeo secured a brief from Rome giving him the authority to relieve members of religious orders from their vow of obedience so that they could serve the sick.

Armed with a series of other grievances, Borromeo removed the Society as administrators of the diocesan seminary in 1579. As far as he was concerned, all clergy within the diocese should be under his authority; the independence of religious orders in areas such as preaching, pastoral work, and confessions did not align with his vision for Tridentine reform. For their part, the Jesuits were equally exasperated by what they perceived to be Borromeo's encroachment upon their independence, something at the heart of their effectiveness within the Catholic Reformation. As Giovanni Battista Peruschi, SJ, superior at San Fedele church in Milan, noted in a letter to the Jesuit general, Everard Mercurian, in 1577: 'The major trouble is with the Cardinal, who does not understand or like the manner and the spirit of the Society.'

That is not to say that Borromeo was ill disposed towards religious orders; he hailed Capuchin bravery during the outbreak of pestilence. The Capuchins threw themselves into ministering to the sick and dying, with significant numbers themselves perishing. Some historians have even speculated that, as two driving forces of the Catholic Reformation, the Capuchins never received the hostility that the Jesuits did, at least partly due to their self-sacrifice during the pandemic. Borromeo was certainly not the only person to have concerns about the novelty of Jesuit structures and call for their reform; it is perhaps revealing that Borromeo, who died in 1584, was canonized in 1612 (Figure 2), but Ignatius of Loyola, who died in 1556, was not canonized until 1622.

What is vital is that the Borromean model for Tridentine Catholicism was admired and consciously imitated by others across Europe and the world, albeit with regional adaptations. As the Observant Franciscan Francesco Panigarola put it during his funeral oration, the example of Borromeo's life made him 'fit for

25

2. Print depicting the life of Charles Borromeo (Italian, *c*.1604).

that great undertaking to which God called him for the reformation of the universal world'. His was one strong vision of Catholic reform, fully endorsed by the Church, but very different from other equally acceptable programmes. Milan's plague years showed how these different visions might clash.

Religious orders—reforming the old and creating the new, part 2

Trent did not mark the end of reform within religious orders. For example, the Franciscan and Augustinian recollect movements, which emphasized strict observance of the rule, had their roots in pre-Trent days, but really took off in the late 16th and early 17th centuries. Similarly, the Discalced Carmelite movement blossomed for both men and women. They followed an austere observance of Carmelite life, devoted to meditation and mortifications such as fasting, as witnessed in the adoption of the term 'discalced', literally meaning they wore no footwear. Elsewhere, the Benedictine congregation of Saint-Maur in France—the Maurists—was confirmed in 1621 and heralded the revival of the old tradition of monastic scholarship.

This mobilizing energy also created new orders. Among these were the Piarists, who from the early years of the 17th century devoted themselves to the provision of free education for poor boys. Just prior to his death in 1550, the Spaniard John of God constructed a hospital in Granada; after papal recognition in 1572 the Hospitallers of St John of God took a special vow to care for the sick. Similar work was carried out by the Camillians, founded in Rome by Camillus de Lellis in 1584. Associations of priests who never took traditional monastic vows, but lived together in community following the evangelical counsels of poverty, chastity, and obedience, while under the jurisdiction of the local bishop, also flourished. The most famous examples were the Oratory of Philip Neri in Rome, which received papal recognition in 1575, and the Oratory transplanted to France by Pierre de Bérulle in 1611. Also in France, Vincent de Paul's Congregation of the Mission (known as the Lazarists) came into being in 1625, dedicated to rural preaching missions and clerical formation.

Women religious were also part of this great tide of spiritual renewal. Perhaps the most significant group pushing at the boundaries of traditional approaches to religious life were the Ursulines. Founded by a Franciscan tertiary Angela Merici in 1535, she and her companions in the Company of the Servants of St Ursula performed good works, assisting with hospitals and orphanages around Brescia in Italy. Merici's vision was for a community of virgins and widows serving 'in the world' as had happened in the Early Church; it received papal confirmation in 1544. In 1567, Borromeo brought the Ursulines to Milan to help with his programme of lay religious instruction and by 1576 required all bishops living within his province to invite them into their dioceses. It was he who introduced the common life and simple vows to the Ursulines but, perhaps most significantly, directed them towards the schooling, especially of girls, for which they would become famous. However, their way of life caused disquiet and was put under social as well as religious pressure: in 17th-century France, for example, the Ursulines followed strict enclosure and made solemn vows, which differed from how they operated elsewhere.

The Visitandines or Visitation nuns were founded in France by the widow Jane Frances Fremiot de Chantel at the encouragement of Francis de Sales. Initially working in the service of the poor and the sick, by 1618 they accepted the requirement for the enclosed life after pressure from the archbishop of Lyon and dedicated themselves to educating young girls in boarding schools. By 1641, they boasted 86 convents in the French-speaking world. Led by Louise de Marillac from 1634, the Daughters of Charity worked alongside Vincent de Paul in caring for the poor and sick in France. They were approved as an order in 1656. Alix le Clerc founded the Congregation of Notre Dame as an unenclosed teaching order in Lorraine, which received papal approval in 1618; in just over 20 years it had grown to 48 houses, spreading across France and Germany. More controversial was the Institute of the Blessed Virgin, founded by the English exile Mary Ward in Saint-Omer,

France, in 1609. Modelled on the Jesuit rule, the fledgling group was welcomed by some but condemned by others, before being officially dissolved in 1631 because it refused to accept enclosure. However, the movement lived on as the English Ladies, running girls' schools in places like Bavaria, where it was under the patronage of significant laity, including members of the ruling Wittelsbach dynasty.

Such examples may give the impression that women religious chafed against the strict rules of enclosure laid out in early December 1563, at the 25th session of the Council of Trent. As mentioned earlier, there had been a great deal of reform aimed at bishops and secular clergy but here, belatedly, the council had reached the religious orders. It was decreed that all communities of female religious should be enclosed (as well as male monastics). The final decree read that 'no nun shall after her profession be permitted to go out of the monastery, even for a brief period under any pretext whatever, except for a lawful reason to be approved by the bishop ... Neither shall anyone, of whatever birth or condition, sex or age, be permitted ... to enter the enclosure of the monastery without the written permission of the bishop.' This ruling was affirmed three years later by Pope Pius V.

This may appear to modern readers as a Church-led attack on women and, indeed, there are well-reported cases of the enforced enclosure of those who did not want it and had previously lived in 'open' convents, particularly in Italy. While strict enclosure appears harsh, and recognizing that the early modern world could hardly be viewed as a beacon of gender equality, we should consider the intentions of the Catholic Reformation. The council fathers themselves noted that all they were doing was renewing the constitution of Pope Boniface VIII, passed in 1298 and known as *Periculoso*; in other words, the intent was spiritual reform and it was clear that some convents, especially in Italy, were playing a social rather than a religious role, primarily used as elite dumping grounds for younger daughters. Those women naturally reacted against the rules of enclosure as, essentially, they had no religious vocation and did not wish to live the life expected of a nun. In the case of Venice, forced vocations were linked to cases of ill-discipline in convents. Tellingly, rules about enclosure went hand in hand with guidance to ensure each would-be nun had a true vocation and was not being forced to enter the convent. In other words, this was all about reform of the religious life; those who were involved in convents for secular convenience were always going to be against enclosure.

It is therefore more revealing to consider the far greater number of willing nuns, as opposed to the unwilling. Markedly, they appear to have embraced the committed life of enclosure. Perhaps the most famous example is the Carmelite Teresa of Avila. Dissatisfied at the laxity of her own convent, she started the reform branch known as the Discalced Carmelites, who followed strict enclosure and led an ascetical life. Such was the impact of Teresa's reform programme that it inspired similar male efforts, such as those of the Spanish Carmelite mystic John of the Cross. The Discalced Carmelites opened their first convent in France at Paris in 1601; within 40 years, there were 55 across that country. Indeed, 17th-century France witnessed an explosion in the numbers of women religious, to the point where they outnumbered male religious for the first time in history. In Paris alone there were around 50 new convents founded in the first half of the 17th century. Enclosure, paradoxically, did not mean being completely cut off from the outside world, as convents recognized their value as prayer factories of the Catholic Reformation. For Teresa of Avila, prayer was an active vocation demanding total spiritual and bodily commitment; for her, enclosure was liberating in that it allowed women to escape worldly entanglements and focus on this vital task.

Expressions of female religious life were often nuanced. For example, although Mary Ward is best known for her vision of unenclosed religious life, she did not reject enclosed observance as a valid option, having first founded a Poor Clare community in Gravelines. In other words, she could see the value of it, even if she grew to discover that that vocation was not for her. Equally, the problems she ran into were at least partly the result of societal context, her vision the target of misogynistic attacks by both Protestants and Catholics opposed to the Jesuit way of life. Nevertheless, her movement survived because men and women valued and supported it, creating regional variations which allowed such initiatives to operate. Laywomen, especially the wealthier, were often significant champions of women religious: for example, Madame Acarie and Madame de Saule-Beuve were both active in introducing the strictly enclosed Discalced Carmelites, as well as the pioneering Ursulines, to Paris. Other groups of women religious found workarounds in the face of opposition. The Daughters of Charity, for example, took private vows meaning they were not considered canonically professed religious, so did not need to be enclosed. As a result, un-cloistered female religious life grew rapidly by the end of the 17th century, regardless of official pronouncements. What really mattered was local backing, whether secular or ecclesiastical, underlining that Catholic reform was not just a centralized impulse. Women's participation in the Catholic Reformation shows how important the local and regional could be.

Chapter 3
Catholic Europe?

The Catholic Reformation needed to secure, and even create, a Catholic Europe, and there were a number of different visions of how best to achieve it. This chapter covers what are traditionally viewed as the heartlands of the Catholic Reformation, but underlines that, even here, the reformers had a lot of work to do in reversing the Protestant advance of the preceding years. Opening with an overview of events in Spain, Portugal, and the Italian states, the chapter then shifts to sites of a more contested reformation. Starting with the Low Countries, the focus then moves to France and its wars of religion, as well as the areas beset by the Thirty Years War—Germany, Austria, and Bohemia—before ending with the Balkan regions and the Polish–Lithuanian Commonwealth. Taken together, these examples underline that nothing was inevitable about the success of shoring up Catholicism in these lands; in fact, that the Catholic Reformation halted swathes of defections to Protestantism in these areas was an achievement, even if it involved a variety of methods not necessarily linked to the Catholic reform movement itself.

Spain

Spain ultimately provided much of the Catholic Reformation's man- and, to some extent, firepower despite extolling a very particular expression of the movement. Indeed, the Spanish understanding of the Catholic Reformation was rooted in events and initiatives that significantly pre-dated the Council of Trent. The end of Moorish rule in the Iberian peninsula with the capture of Granada in 1492 was the catalyst, this historical moment fuelling a Spanish understanding of itself as a Catholic champion, its identity inseparably tied with the faith. Catholic orthodoxy—at least as it was understood within Spain—became the defining national characteristic. It gave rise to the Inquisition particularly prominent in the Iberian world, as the pope had given Catholic monarchs authority over the institution in those lands in 1483. The 15th century saw increasing persecution of the Jews in Spain and it is no coincidence that, as Muslim enclaves were pushed out, 1492 also witnessed the expulsion of the Jews. This combined with a growing belief, underscored by several laws, in the need for 'pure bloodlines' for certain ecclesiastical and political posts, resulting in an obsession with the supposed enemy within.

A particular focus of the Inquisition was *conversos*: those with Jewish backgrounds whose families had converted to Catholicism. It was suspected that they still harboured Jewish sympathies and beliefs, and that these could harm the 'pure blood' of the nation. To this list was added *moriscos*, that is, those of Moorish descent whose families had at some point been baptized. Spanish paranoia saw the Inquisition testing these people for hidden Islamic sympathies, resulting in their wholesale banishment from Spain in 1609. Unlike much of mainland Europe, there was very little evidence of Protestantism in Spain. However, there was public panic when two tiny Protestant networks were discovered in the mid-1550s, resulting in all sorts of people falling under suspicion of being heretics; even the primate of Spain—the archbishop of Toledo—was arrested by the Inquisition during this scare. The Inquisition is discussed in Chapter 5; for now, it is important to note its peculiarity to the Iberian world. Spanish Catholicism created the environment for the Inquisition due to its specific national self-understanding and identity. It was a land where heresy was associated with foreign interests and rebellion.

That connection was because of another defining characteristic of Spanish Catholicism: the monarch had the right to nominate all bishops and heads of religious orders in Spain. Philip II was king for most of the second half of the 16th century. Fully committed to Catholicism, he even constructed a palace, known as the Escorial, that acted as both a Habsburg family mausoleum and a monastery. Equally, he was intensely aware of his role as a Catholic monarch, not only in his own kingdom, but also in defending Christendom both within and, in particular, without the Mediterranean arena against the Ottoman Turks. In other words, Spain was a self-consciously Catholic nation. Its bishops were at the forefront of the reform party at the Council of Trent, intent on battling what they considered the self-interested, decadent representatives of the Roman curia. However, this criticism was as patriotic as it was reformist, an expression of the Spanish belief that their way of doing things was the true Catholicism and the right way of achieving Catholic reform. In many ways, given his power over the Church, Philip acted as a mini-pope. Indeed in 1572 the Spanish government declared null and void all appeals to Rome from the ecclesiastical courts, an act not dissimilar to those passed in Protestant states.

All that being said, Spanish Catholicism should not simply be understood as a repressive movement. It was a very religious society and there was genuine spiritual fervour. Philip II was quick to order the promulgation of the Tridentine decrees in Spain and for them to be acted upon. For example, 23 seminaries were founded between 1564 and 1610. Significant efforts were made on the home missionary front to spread and increase religious knowledge among the laity. Admittedly, this may have helped nurture a common religious bond around which the nation could unite, but it also represented genuine effort at reform. There was much charitable support for the founding of hospitals, poor relief, and new religious institutions. Over half of all the books published in Spain between 1500 and 1670 were religious in focus, with many in the vernacular in order to reach a broad public readership.

It is not surprising that a number of the new religious orders sprang from Spain, such as the Jesuits, whose first three generals were all from the Iberian peninsula. Interestingly, Diego Laínez, the second Jesuit general who played a major role at the Council of Trent, was from a family with a *converso* background, as were other major Catholic Reformation figures, including Teresa of Avila and John of the Cross. It is certainly notable that both the Jesuits and the Discalced Carmelites opposed the pure blood statutes. It is also no surprise that Spanish Catholicism was tinged with apocalyptic ideas, believing it was the nation's divine task to evangelize the world. When efforts at this failed, the whole nation blamed its own sins and undertook penance. It is certainly an irony of the Catholic Reformation that one of its greatest proponents with a global empire was so suspicious of 'new Christians'.

Portugal

The Portuguese experience of the Catholic Reformation was very similar to that of the Spanish. It was one of the first countries to officially promulgate the Tridentine decrees, with the archbishop of Braga, Bartolomeu dos Martires, a champion of change at the Council of Trent, regardless of the fact that the measures he backed cost him in terms of wealth. Not for nothing was Charles Borromeo greatly impressed by the bishop during a trip to Rome. As with Spain, there was genuine renewal in the country: nearly 170 new religious houses were founded between 1550 and 1650; seven new diocesan seminaries were opened by 1700; while a major intellectual figure like the Spanish Jesuit Francisco Suárez held a chair in Theology at the University of Coimbra.

On one level, none of this was surprising. After the death of King Sebastian in a crusade against Morocco, the Spanish and Portuguese crowns were unified from 1580 to 1640. Under this system, the link between the ruler and the Church became even more explicit than in Spain, through figures such as Pedro de Castilho, bishop of Leiria, who served two terms as viceroy as well as a decade as inquisitor general at the start of the 17th century. In addition, the episcopacy was overwhelmingly drawn from the ranks of the nobility. Moreover, the Inquisition in Portugal shared the same fixation on those of Jewish ancestry. However, the tight bond between national identity and Catholicism had an unexpected extra incentive: growing resentment of Spanish imperial ambitions at the expense of Portugal. In this case, Catholicism increasingly helped the nation assert itself against Spain, for example in arguing for the ecclesiastical primacy of Braga in the Iberian peninsula. All this fed into the revolt against Spain in 1640. A once-more independent Portugal further fuelled a common Iberian messianic spur to spread their version of Catholicism to the world, particularly through the Jesuits' missionary work in Asia (the pope having placed the mission under Portuguese influence).

Italian states

Spain's power was also evident in the Italian peninsula, with viceroys running Naples, Sicily, and Milan in the name of the Spanish king, who was also patron of the Medici family in Florence. Some of the Italian states similarly saw the Catholic Reformation fight against heresy as closely linked to combating potential political dissent and ensuring the loyalty of the populace. Even so, there was significant variation in the course of the Catholic Reformation in the Italian peninsula, particularly between the northern states and those in the south. Notably, these mirrored several of the different approaches to achieving Catholic reform outlined in the previous chapter.

Charles Borromeo provided the model of bishop-led, diocesan reform in the north of the region, as well as showing what Tridentine episcopal renewal could look like. Figures such as Gabriele Paleotti, archbishop of Bologna, attempted similar patterns of renewal, as well as Agostino Valier, bishop of Verona, who encouraged lay piety, penning a manual for devout women.

None of these figures copied Borromeo exactly, but adapted his approach for the areas in which they worked, practising their own form of mild accommodation with local traditions more commonly seen on the fringes of global Catholicism. Several of the new religious orders emerged from the Italian states, as the Catholic Reformation witnessed the outreach of institutional charity towards those on the margins, from orphans to prostitutes and prisoners, with equal attention paid to the reform of behaviour and morality. Lay elites played a vital role and, as we have seen, their support was instrumental to the success of the new religious orders aimed at spiritual renewal and charity. Meanwhile, seminaries were gradually constructed to better educate and improve the clergy.

Reforming bishops were also active in the south of the peninsula. The celebrated Jesuit intellectual Robert Bellarmine sought to implement the Tridentine decrees in the poorer region of Capua, embarking on a vigorous programme of teaching, preaching, and parish visitations. Another champion of reform in the late 16th century was the archbishop of Taranto, Lelio Brancaccio. However, the going was harder in the south, particularly where pre-Trent practices meant local elites held the right to nominate parish priests, thus shielding substandard clergy from episcopal discipline. This hampered attempts to halt clerical concubinage and improve the standard of the clergy. Moreover, the area was unquestionably impoverished, with most wealth and status centred on Naples. For these reasons, the south became the focus of Catholic reform driven by religious orders undertaking missionary work among the rural population. Pioneered by the likes of the Lazarists and the Jesuits, these countryside preaching missions undertook catechesis and encouraged spiritual reform, laying the foundations for a new wave of reforming bishops in the southern regions in the latter half of the 17th century.

Overall, the populace of the Italian peninsula was largely receptive to Catholic reform. This renewal was social as well as religious;

it even encompassed the role of parents (especially mothers) in conveying the faith to their children. Parish priests emphasized parental responsibilities, which were also the focus of a posthumously published address by Federico Borromeo, archbishop of Milan. As with the Spanish example, some of this Catholic Reformation could be tainted by proximity to the state's secular aims but, overall, there was a thoroughgoing attempt at the Catholic reformation of the religious, the social, and even the public spheres, with no limit to its scope.

Low Countries

From what was a war-scarred beginning, the southern provinces of the Low Countries went on to become a beacon of the Catholic Reformation. The Dutch Revolt against Spanish domination was vicious and bloody, resulting in the northern provinces forming the Protestant Dutch Republic and the southern—constituting modern-day Belgium, Luxembourg, and parts of northern France—remaining under Catholic Habsburg rule. It was not until 1598 that real Catholic reform started to gain pace when Philip II's daughter, Isabella Clara Eugenia, became co-regent with her husband, Archduke Albert of Austria. Re-Catholicization was rapid; in 1581, during the revolt, Catholic practice had been banned in Antwerp, but by the 17th century it was a bastion of the Catholic Reformation, a global printing hub for its works, and a pioneer of baroque artistic endeavour through the likes of Peter Paul Rubens.

Isabella and Albert were great patrons of the new religious orders, such as the Franciscan Recollects, and they introduced the Discalced Carmelites from Spain. There were nearly 1,000 Capuchins in the region by 1620, while there were more than 1,500 Jesuits by 1626. To give an idea of how significant a number this was, the Jesuits in Spain—birthplace of the order and a far bigger country—numbered just under 3,000 at the same time. Isabella was a great supporter of female religious, including the English convents in exile. Following her husband's death in 1621, she donned the habit of a Franciscan tertiary. Catholic reform in the area became a model for others to emulate, as secular and religious authorities worked towards a common goal. This could lead to a blurring of divisions, such as secular courts' involvement in religious matters, but it never went as far as Spain, as the co-regents did not allow the Inquisition to function in the area. Clerical standards were raised by regular bishops' visitations; lay membership of confraternities was high, as was attendance at catechism classes for children and reception of holy communion; the universities at Leuven and Douai were standard bearers of Catholic Reformation learning; while exile communities from Britain and Ireland established bases in the area from which missionary activity could be launched to their Protestant homelands.

France

France spent much of the early modern period battling with Spain to be considered the global superpower, and like Spain it had its own, often idiosyncratic, relationship with Catholicism. Its most dominant strand was what is often termed Gallican Catholicism. This had its roots in the conciliarist movement mentioned in the previous chapter, but the most pertinent point for the French context was that it limited Rome's influence on ecclesiastical appointments. By the early 16th century, the French monarchy had the majority of major benefices in its power, including hundreds of monastic houses and the appointment of most bishops. Technically, the pope retained a right of refusal on any nominations the king made, but in reality, royal power held sway. Though fully in communion with the pope, French Catholicism was thus tied closely to the monarch and the nation, self-consciously intent on defending what it considered the liberties of the French Church in relation to Rome. This meant that, technically, the decrees of the Council of Trent were never officially accepted in France as they were considered to infringe upon the Gallican rights.

This is part of the reason why the period of Catholic Reformation did not really start until well into the 17th century in France. Perhaps even more important was that the nation spent most of the second half of the 16th century engaged in what was effectively a bloody civil war. Known as the wars of religion and starting in the early 1560s, French society became increasingly fractured as a growing wave of Calvinist conversions saw the Huguenots challenge the nation's Catholic identity. The throne emerged as the ultimate prize. Conflict was savage, including the notorious St Bartholomew's Day Massacre on 24 August 1572, when Catholics in Paris slaughtered their Protestant neighbours. The Catholic League stood against perceived Huguenot gains; allied with Spain, it valued religious allegiance over national, thus rejecting the Gallican approach. The main phase of the wars of religion was brought to an uneasy end when the Calvinist Henri of Navarre ascended the throne having converted to Catholicism, allegedly commenting that Paris was worth a Mass. In 1598 he passed the Edict of Nantes, which granted toleration of the Huguenots while recognizing Catholic primacy in the country.

Despite surviving a number of assassination attempts—including by a former student of the Jesuits (consequently, the Jesuits were temporarily banished from France)—Henri IV was killed by a Catholic fanatic in 1610. This led to a revival of Gallican principles and a rejection of papal power. Henri was succeeded by his son, Louis XIII, but as he was a child the country was governed under regency by his mother, Marie de' Medici. The queen mother became a focal point for those of the Catholic League who sought a pro-Spanish foreign policy, the aim being to create a united Catholic front against Protestants of all stripes. Support for this position grew during the Franco-Spanish wars of the 1620s and 1630s as France allied itself with Protestant countries such as the Dutch Republic and Gustavus Adolphus of Sweden against the

Habsburgs. Several Huguenot rebellions in the same period saw Protestant rebels in, for example, Languedoc destroy Catholic churches, kill priests, and terrorize the local Catholic lay population, only further fuelling the tense situation.

It was at this unstable juncture that Catholic reform was kickstarted in France. Thanks to Alexandre Dumas's 19th-century novel *The Three Musketeers*, Cardinal Richelieu has the reputation of a scheming villain, yet in his position as first minister from 1624 to 1642 he worked alongside Louis XIII to stabilize France. Richelieu embodied a particularly French interpretation of the Catholic Reformation, where bishops were reformers but also political agents because of the Gallican Church's connection to royal and noble patronage. Although Richelieu was appointed to a bishopric that was in the patronage of his family—that of Luçon in 1607 at the age of only 22—he summoned a diocesan synod, embarked on parish visitations, explored founding a seminary to reform the clergy, and penned a short catechism that was subsequently translated into a number of different languages. By 1624 he had risen to the level of first minister, and firmly identified the Church's interests with those of the French state, writing in his *Political Testament*, 'the first foundation of the welfare of a state was the establishment of the reign of God'. His Gallican vision of reformed French Catholicism saw off the Catholic League's opposition as he worked to halt Habsburg dominance of Europe and raise Louis back to what he considered the king of France's rightful position of prominence among the Christian monarchs.

By this time, the Catholic Reformation in France had three aims: reform the decadence that had set in, particularly in religious life; Catholicize the French people, especially in the countryside; and push back against the Huguenots, whose significant number meant France had become a religiously plural society. The new international religious orders of the Catholic Reformation played a vital role in achieving the first aim. The Capuchins and the

Jesuits were at the forefront of these efforts, joined by the likes of the Ursulines, the Oratorians, and the Discalced Carmelite nuns of Teresa of Avila's reform, the last two introduced to France and given a national spin by Cardinal Pierre de Bérulle, who was also a patron of Vincent de Paul. Nor were the older orders ignored; for example, the Cluniac reform of the Benedictines thrived. Reform of French professed life had a major influence on the religious character of the country. For example, Margaret Mary Alacoque, a Visitandine nun in the second half of the 17th century, helped spread a strong devotion to the Sacred Heart that would come to be a defining characteristic of French Catholicism.

Although the rise of female teaching congregations was a challenge to the Tridentine rules of enclosure, their eventual acceptance in France as the 17th century wore on was, as historian Elizabeth Rapley has commented, 'the triumph of one set of Tridentine values over another'. The Catholic Reformation may on the one hand have been about a reassertion of rules such as enclosure, but on the other, the council had also stressed the need to instruct the laity and, in the face of Protestant challenge in France, this value prevailed. Knowledge of the faith became the watchword. As such, female religious life, both contemplative and active, boomed in France.

The orders also played a major role in the Catholicization of the nation. Much of the country outside Paris was viewed as a field for missionary work, due to ignorance of the faith, but also because large areas were particularly scarred by the wars of religion and had a significant or majority Protestant population. The Capuchins and the Jesuits took the lead as they so frequently did in the global Catholic Reformation. Work was undertaken to found seminaries across the country, one of the most famous being that of Saint-Sulpice in Issy-les-Moulineaux in 1641. It was staffed by the Sulpicians, a new religious community, who, along with the Lazarists inspired by Vincent de Paul, specialized in clerical training and ran most French seminaries by 1700. In the countryside, many women responded positively to the charitable and spiritual action promoted by these reformed priests and the values they placed upon family responsibility. The intensity of Catholic reform in Paris was exceptional, including the founding of major religious houses such as the nuns of Port-Royal, the poor relief of Vincent de Paul and his followers, and the education of Catholic Reformation clergy at the Sorbonne. By the second half of the century, catechism schools were being rolled out across the country.

All this activity went hand in hand with pushing back against the Huguenots. Persuasion rather than coercion was the policy of Richelieu and his successor Cardinal Mazarin. Common methods included sending in the Capuchins to preach to the poor, the Jesuits to attract the nobility, and the Ursulines to educate the girls. Richelieu, during his time at Luçon, had utilized the Capuchins to convert the Protestant populace in the area, though he viewed semi-toleration of the Huguenots as good for the state after the years of conflict and, in the long term, good for advancing the Catholic Reformation. In the wake of the Huguenot rebellions in the 17th century, loyalty to France was increasingly tied to Catholicism and, with the application of various small pressures, increasing numbers of Protestant nobles converted to Catholicism to prove their loyalty and gain office.

Although this may sound similar to the Spanish approach, it never went to the extreme of pronouncing a clear link between heresy and political treason. In the eyes of the French Gallican Church, these long-term efforts bore fruit under the glory of the Sun King, Louis XIV, who in 1685 revoked the Edict of Nantes and withdrew toleration of Protestantism. Catholic practice rates were once again high, but, as ever in the Catholic Reformation, anxiety remained among its most committed proponents about how much internal spiritual reform had been achieved. As one of the nation's most famous preachers, the Jesuit Louis

Bourdaloue, noted, there was a difference between reception of the sacraments out of habit and social expectation and 'receiving them in a holy way, which means that we must receive them with a real compassion of heart'.

Central and eastern Europe

Germany was the birthplace of the Protestant Reformation. Though it did not have a nationally focused Church like that of France, its secular princes held a significant amount of power, including over the appointment to some bishoprics and benefices, meaning it was no surprise that Luther had appealed to them to reform the Church. Reaction to the challenge was slow; it was not only Protestant reformers who opposed any attempt at Catholic Reformation, but also the vested interests upon which the imperial system was built, with the Catholic elite, as elsewhere in Europe, using church offices as family property. The Peace of Augsburg, signed in 1555 between the Holy Roman Emperor Charles V and the Schmalkaldic League of Lutheran princes, broadly allowed the ruler of a region to dictate its religion. As a result, the Holy Roman Empire was in danger of collapse: Protestant electors were set to outnumber Catholic, while most of northern Germany had become Protestant. In Bohemia around 90 per cent of the population had abandoned Catholicism by 1600. The Peace of Augsburg meant that secular princes effectively controlled the Church in their lands, so dictated not only the confessionalization of the geographical area, but also the reform—both Protestant and Catholic—of a region's churches. In 1618, the Bohemian Rebellion—in which Protestant leaders of the area rejected the new Catholic Emperor Ferdinand II by defenestrating his representatives at the palace in Prague—started the Thirty Years War. Two years later, the Bohemian Protestant forces were defeated by the Catholic League at the battle of White Mountain just outside Prague. Emperor Ferdinand's re-Catholicization of the area was brutal, with executions, banishments, and property confiscations.

Even areas that had remained largely Catholic, such as Bavaria and Austria, experienced forceful tactics. But just as Protestantism gained from secular princes deciding an area's religious character, so too with Catholicism. A member of the Catholic Wittelsbach family, Maximilian of Bavaria, governed from 1598 to 1651. Within the first year of his reign, he passed the Law of Morality and Religion—also typical of Protestant princes in the region—that, among other things, encouraged lay reception of holy communion at Easter, forbade crossing borders to attend Protestant services, and denounced clerics breaking their vow of chastity. Moreover, certificates attesting to Mass attendance, reception of communion, and practice of confession were introduced. Nevertheless, Maximilian was also pragmatic; he supported the Peace of Westphalia in 1648 that brought an end to the Thirty Years War and took a step towards religious pluralism and toleration at state level by recognizing the right of princes to choose Protestantism.

Following the signing of the peace, there was a steady stream of conversions to Catholicism in order to secure Habsburg patronage. However, a top-down approach focused on the leaders of the region neglects Catholic ecclesiastical reform efforts, particularly the preaching missions of the Capuchins and the Jesuits. Put simply, there was authentic renewal, which resulted in several regions consolidating their Catholic character. As in France, interconfessional conflict delayed the Catholic Reformation in the area and it did not really get going till well into the 17th century: the Roman missal of the Tridentine liturgy was not published in Cologne until the mid-1620s. The Jesuits played a vital if somewhat fabled role in the re-Catholicization of central Europe, having been invited to Cologne as early as 1544, a city which became one of their strongholds. As ever, that does not mean there was no opposition to their approach, and, of course, other ways existed of interpreting Catholic Reformation. More pointedly, there was wider recognition within the transnational Church that the lands of the Holy Roman Empire were not able to reform themselves: the Collegium Germanicum et Hungaricum was founded in Rome in 1552 under the direction of the Jesuits to train clergy in the new Tridentine ways and to school secular officials.

By 1630, there were five Jesuit provinces in the Holy Roman Empire consisting of roughly 3,000 members. Emperor Ferdinand II was the product of a Jesuit school, as was Maximilian of Bavaria, who showed genuine spiritual commitment. He brought both the Capuchins and the Jesuits to Bavaria and cultivated the image of the pious prince, a particularly strong tradition in Austria. It is no coincidence that the imperial crypt in Vienna, resting place of the Habsburgs since the 17th century, is in a Capuchin church. In short, reformation of the clergy and the laity pushed through the Catholic Reformation against entrenched interests and reversed the tide of Protestant advance. Progress was made, once again, thanks to the new religious orders harnessing all the tools of the Catholic Reformation, from education to theatre and music (see Chapter 6), coupled with the re-energized spiritual commitment of the laity. These lands witnessed major activity, building upon pre-existing practices but rechannelling them through a Tridentine lens, such as the revival of pilgrimages, especially to the imperial shrine of Mary at Altötting. The area was united by a revived Catholic identity, brought about by evangelization and improved clerical standards. The Catholic Reformation in these regions may have gone hand in hand with territorial restitution, but it was secured by assiduous religious renewal and it was ultimately a remarkable turnaround.

Even more complex were the areas under Ottoman rule. In 1526, Ottoman military success effectively decapitated Catholicism in Hungary, and Protestantism swept into the void. The situation fast became dire: between 1573 and 1596, even the position of archbishop of Esztergom, the nation's primatial see, was infrequently filled. Once again, the Catholic Reformation looked to the religious orders to reverse the Church's fortunes: Jesuits and different shades of Franciscans drawn from several nations started to re-Catholicize the area. This included the part of Hungary occupied by the Ottomans until the 1690s, which was considered missionary territory; a second wave of Catholic Reformation would follow the reunification of the country. Parts of Ottoman-occupied Hungary segued into the wider Balkan regions and came under the Church's global missionary leadership.

The major actors here were the Bosnian Franciscan Friars Minor, who considered it their role to maintain the region's identity while under Ottoman rule. The friars' local approach to Catholicism saw them clash with the Rome-backed Jesuit mission to the area. Nevertheless, the Franciscans started to send Bosnian friars for education in Rome, exposing them to the ideas of the Catholic Reformation, and by the mid-17th century all missionary bishops active in the Turkish Balkans were drawn from their number. Significant problems persisted, largely due to the lack of an educational network and the fact that the numbers of priests were small despite external missionary efforts. In addition, Albania represented a 'failure' of the Catholic Reformation as its population gradually turned to Islam, the religion of the new rulers.

Polish–Lithuanian Commonwealth

Unlike in much of Europe, religious toleration and pluralism were the hallmarks of the nobility who dominated the Polish–Lithuanian Commonwealth. The region contained communities of Catholics, Lutherans, Calvinists, Orthodox, Anabaptists, and Unitarians, as well as several other groups. By the mid-16th century, various shades of Protestantism had made decent headway, with a sixth of the nobility professing themselves as such. Some mild attempts at Catholic reform were made, but it was not until Cardinal Stanislaus Hosius returned to Poland (after playing a key role in the final sessions of the Council of Trent) that the Catholic Reformation truly got under way. Through him, Poland became one of the first states to accept the decrees of Trent and implement its programmes of reform. Seminaries were introduced to train clergy not only for parish work, but also for missionary activity among the non-Catholic population. There was the occasional outbreak of mild violence, but it was small compared to elsewhere, and persuasion seems to have been used more than coercion.

Notable converts included Mikołaj Krzysztof Radziwiłł, leader of the Protestant community, who was inspired to convert to Catholicism by Hosius and the Jesuit Piotr Skarga. It was Hosius who introduced the Jesuits to the region in 1564, and they played a major role in training a new breed of ecclesiastical and secular leadership at their institutions in Rome and Poland. A more assertive Catholicism was ushered in by King Stephen Báthory (who ruled 1576–86) as the Polish monarchy increasingly became associated with the Jesuits; indeed, John II Casimir Vasa (ruled 1648–68) ascended the throne having been granted dispensation to leave his Jesuit vows. Gradually, as elsewhere, Polish national identity fused with Catholicism.

Nevertheless, it was the mendicants who arguably had more influence on the laity than the Jesuits. For example, the Dominicans vastly outnumbered the Jesuits, their spirituality encouraging female piety, as women dominated their confraternities of the Holy Rosary. Convent life was remodelled, by, for example, the reformed Benedictine rule of the abbess of Chelmo, Magdalena Mortęska, which by 1650 had been adopted by 20 convents with more than 800 members. Women acted as significant patrons of these Catholic Reformation initiatives, which drew on international influences. Teresa of Avila's works were in print and circulating by the final years of the 16th century, and the Discalced Carmelites arrived the following decade, initially staffed by Spanish and Italians. In addition, the Observant Franciscans (known as Bernardines in the region) played a major role in preaching, while the Theatines and Piarists provided education. As elsewhere, different visions of Catholic reform existed and the religious orders sometimes clashed; indeed, the Capuchins were not introduced in great numbers until the end of the 17th century in order to avoid just such contention.

Chapter 4
Missionaries and martyrs

Europe may have been the starting point for the Catholic Reformation and its missionary impulse, but the movement can only truly be understood if we examine it globally. There was a dual aspect to the missionary Catholic Reformation, which on occasion led to conflict over how best to pursue it, particularly on the peripheries of Catholic Europe. One thrust of missionary endeavour was evangelization of the New World and areas previously not exposed to Christianity. This field included large areas of the Americas that were part of the Iberian empire, as well as the continents of Africa, and, perhaps most importantly, Asia. Europe's imagination was gripped by tales of China and Japan. Lay Catholics were captivated by stories of missionaries in far off, newly discovered lands, for whose edification they were written. Equally, these reports were packed with danger, with the threat of martyrdom hanging over those depicted as brave pioneers.

Simultaneously, Catholic Europe did not have to look far for its own more local martyrdoms. These men and women were presented as proof of the evils of Protestantism and highlighted the other facet of missionary endeavour at this time: the reclaiming of formerly Catholic lands now lost to heresy. Although there were martyrs in the Low Countries, Ireland, and Scotland, it was England where they featured most prominently. The persecuted Catholics of that kingdom were presented as heroes of the Catholic

Reformation, put before a European audience to attract international support while simultaneously strengthening spiritual commitment. Combined with the then-recent rediscovery of the catacombs in Rome, this persecution pointed towards the religious authenticity of the Catholic Church, St Peter's having been literally built on the blood of the martyrs. In other words, events on the peripheries of Catholic reform shaped the character of Catholicism in its centres.

The Americas

There were different approaches to mission even when seeking to evangelize an area previously not exposed to Christianity. Spain, again, had its own very distinct way of doing things. Confident its version of Catholicism was the only correct way, the nation had a near messianic belief in its responsibility to bring the world to Christ. The Spanish crown had secured papal acceptance of their claim to the new worlds of South America discovered in the late 15th century, which placed on them the obligation to spread Christianity. The monarch interpreted this 'mission' contract as giving them the full rights of conquest. This position was entrenched by the Spanish monarch's right to appoint all bishops. Spanish colonialists thus waged a war on paganism in their self-appointed role as Catholic champions, but to serve their own ends. Official Catholic mission went hand in hand with colonial expansion in the Iberian empire.

Yet it started in a more complex way. The first religious order to have permanent representation on the mainland of South America was the Franciscans. Following their arrival in 1524 in what is now Mexico, crowds turned out to hear them preach and subsequently receive baptism. Practising an early form of inculturation, the friars learnt the local language, resisting a 1550 royal decree that they should teach only in Spanish to the indigenous people. The Franciscan Bernardino de Sahagún was a figurehead of this approach; sympathetic to local traditions and a scholar of the Aztec language, Nahuatl, the 12 books of his *Historia general de las cosas de Nueva España* (now known as the Florentine Codex) documented indigenous culture and were produced in collaboration with locals. Castigating the colonialists for their greed and brutality, the friars prioritized the harvest of souls. For example, Gerónimo de Mendieta recorded the evangelization of the area, but also the abuses of the colonialists in his *Historia eclesiástica Indiana*. He extolled the indigenous people as childlike but devout, and argued that they should not be enslaved. When the Mayans of Yucatan rebelled against Spanish conquest in 1546, it was the Franciscans who protected them from savage reprisals after the rising was crushed, once more using the local language to preach in the area.

Perhaps the most famous critic of colonialist behaviour was the Dominican Bartolomé de las Casas. By the end of his life las Casas was fiercely opposed to all forms of human slavery. Throughout his life he was dogged by accusations of treason against Spain for his denunciations against what he saw happening in the New World. During a brief stint as bishop of Qhiapas from 1543 till his resignation in 1550, he even withheld absolution to slave holders in the confessional, having been inspired by another Dominican, Antonio de Montesinos, who had been among the first to oppose what the Spanish were doing in Hispaniola. Following time spent in Guatemala, las Casas argued that people could not be forced to convert; they must instead have a real grasp and acceptance of the faith.

This latter attitude led him into conflict with the Franciscans, who had adopted a method of baptism en masse. Even among the Franciscan missionaries there were differences of opinion, and some opposed the approach of the likes of de Sahagún. Disease came with the colonialists and their rapid empire-building. The institutional apparatus of bishops and secular clergy also accompanied colonization and this saw the friars' authority decrease. The view rapidly developed that only Hispanicized people were true converts, an opinion held strongly by those born to Spanish parents in the New World, the creoles. Colonialist attitudes came to dominate; at the first two Mexican provincial church councils, it was decreed that indigenous people and those of mixed heritage—the mestizo—could not be ordained priests. The ban was lifted on mestizo by the third council in 1585, but the sentiment only served to make Catholicism look foreign and, more pointedly, Spanish. After a Mayan convert discovered idols in a cave in the 1560s, the Franciscan provincial Diego de Landa took it as proof that the indigenous people were clinging secretly to their old ways, including human sacrifice. De Landa partnered with colonial rulers to instigate full-scale repression and torture. In 1572, he was appointed bishop of Yucatan. Tellingly, the Mayans continued to accept Christianity but increasingly harnessed its apocalyptic teachings, believing that Christ would judge the evil Spanish empire at the end times.

Spanish colonialism eventually crushed the Inca religion in what is now Peru, but at first the missionary effort was, as in Mexico, markedly different (Figure 3). Dominicans also attempted evangelization in the local tongue, founding a college (later a university) in Lima in 1548. As in Mexico, the friars took an interest in local culture; the Dominican Domingo de Santo Tomás published on the grammar and vocabulary of the Quechua language in 1560. Having spent time in Paraguay, where he had learnt the local languages, the Franciscan Francisco Solano arrived in Lima at the start of the 17th century, and promptly set about chastising the Spanish colonialists for betrayal of their baptismal promises.

Catholicism thrived among the Spanish-speaking population. Isabel Flores de Oliva, who had a Spanish-born father and a creole mother, became a Dominican nun; known as Rose of Lima, she would become the first saint born in the New World. Her friend, the Dominican laybrother Martin de Porres, whose mother was a freed slave, was regarded as a saint soon after his

3. A Testerian catechism.

death in 1639. Despite this, Spanish suspicion of indigenous 'superstition' remained. In 1618, the viceroy of Peru closed the Jesuit college to the Indians, while another Jesuit college would go on to be one of the largest slave-holders in the area, and was organized around ideas of class and 'colour'. Between 1641 and 1671, the archbishop of Lima launched a programme of inspections, ostensibly to root out idolatry among the local population, but which soon became another tool of Spanish exploitation.

Similar phenomena can be seen in the Portuguese territories of South America, especially Brazil, where Portuguese rulers had the right to nominate to episcopal sees and colonial ambition rubbed up against Catholic mission. The union of Portugal and Spain from 1580 to 1640 complicated matters, but the Portuguese approach, arguably even more so than Spain's, prioritized trade over the interests of the mission, as will be particularly apparent in discussion of Africa.

Jesuits were relatively late to the New World mission. Arriving after 1570, their members were drawn from a range of countries, so they were never as dominated as the other orders were by Spaniards. By the early 17th century, in their mission to the Guaraní Indians of modern-day Paraguay, the Jesuits had started constructing Indian Christian settlements, known as reductions, where locals could flee to escape colonial exploitation and, more explicitly, Portuguese slave-holders. Acting as protectors from, and middlemen with, the secular authorities, the Jesuits even convinced the colonial rulers that the thousands living in the reductions should be armed to fight off their would-be enslavers. As elsewhere, the missionaries learnt the local language and adapted indigenous rituals to Christian signs and practice. It was not until the 1750s that the reductions were crushed by the Spanish–Portuguese army.

So where does that leave the Catholic Reformation in South America? An old approach to history often painted the Spanish colonial effort as heroic and civilizing, bringing the light of Christ to this new world. Modern scholarship has tended to swing in the opposite direction, generalizing the period as one of violent, forced Christianization. Moreover, as local ways were often mixed with new Catholic practice, some scholars question how much actual Christian doctrine was accepted. Such binary declarations are unlikely to do justice to the reality and are in danger of obliterating the genuine experience of Christianity for large numbers. They neglect personal spiritual experience and run the risk of making judgements on individual consciences. There are examples of indigenous converts chafing at Spanish church restrictions placed upon them, such as in Peru, where Felipe Guaman Poma de Ayala chronicled the brutalism of the Spanish towards the native people. Plus, there were signs of new religious life, such as the Bethlehemite Brothers and Nuns founded in Guatemala in the 1650s to provide medical care to the poor. That is not to ignore regular early modern concerns about syncretism—the blending of indigenous religion with Catholic practice. For example, in the 18th century, the Inquisition in Peru took a far from benign interest in a person who performed the traditional rite of rubbing llama's blood on the foundations of a building to give it strength, in this case a local church.

But on a wider level, how much of what went on in South America can actually be considered part of the Catholic Reformation? After all, the colonization of South America pre-dates the Council of Trent. In fact, actions taken by popes in the 15th century, long before the era of Catholic Reformation, set the scene in this missionary arena, when *patronato* over certain 'new' worlds was granted to the Spanish, including great swathes of the Americas, and the *padroado* to the Portuguese, particularly the Asian territories and those around Africa. Equally, the Council of Trent never actually addressed the issues raised by Iberian behaviour in South America. It was not until 1622 that Pope Gregory XV established the Congregation of Propaganda Fide to deal with such questions as missionary management, abuses, and evangelization. Propaganda was given authority over all overseas missions, which conflicted with the spiritual authority the Iberian powers believed they had been granted; from that point, the missionaries at least theoretically answered to Propaganda, not the Spanish or Portuguese crowns. Unlike the Iberian empire, Propaganda had no interest in the Europeanization of people in the new worlds. In 1659 it issued guidance to missionaries that made clear it was not their task to change the culture of these people unless 'they are evidently contrary to religion and sound morals'. Missionaries were only to introduce them 'to the faith, which does not despise or destroy the manners and customs of any people'. To do so would inspire resistance, particularly if people's behaviour was disparagingly compared to European manners. Therefore, missionaries should 'do your utmost to adapt yourselves to them'.

Essentially, splitting the secular and the spiritual could be difficult, if not impossible. Moreover, those such as the Jesuit José de Acosta, who recognized what was happening in the New World, often reached for that very Catholic Reformation mantra to explain the problem—lack of good training for missionaries. A case, therefore, can be made that when missionaries behaved in accordance with what might be termed the vision of Tridentine Catholicism, they rubbed up against secular, colonial interests. Indeed, it could be argued that much of what happened in South America was almost a throwback to the pre-Tridentine way. This is not to deny that elements within the Iberian Church clearly interpreted the Catholic Reformation differently and yoked it with Spanish colonial aggrandizement. As the 17th century continued, this approach came to dominate and those like Alfonso de la Peña y Montenegro, bishop of Quito in modern-day Ecuador, who argued for the ordination of black and mestizo priests, became lonely voices. Although not true in every case, religious orders and crown-appointed episcopacies did clash over missionary approaches.

By the 17th century, France had established its own foothold on the American continent in New France, part of modern-day Canada. It increasingly came to be viewed as special mission territory for France, with a small group of Franciscan Recollects arriving in 1615, to be followed by a growing number of Jesuits 10 years later. Tensions existed along the same lines: service of the colony and its expansion versus mission to the indigenous population. The Algonquin and Huron peoples were open to the Jesuit missionaries, unlike the Iroquois, who were encouraged in their anti-French position by a rival colonizer, the Protestant English. When war broke out between the Iroquois and the Huron, several Jesuits were martyred in the 1640s, some with extreme cruelty, and the survivors were forced to retreat to the colonial stronghold of French Quebec.

These events underline how colonial competition could affect Catholic mission. Perhaps most notable in this missionary field was the involvement of female religious. Led by Marie Guyart, known in religion as Marie de l'Incarnation, the Ursulines established the first convent and school for girls in North America in 1639. There had initially been resistance to Guyart's plans until, as with other ground-breaking female religious movements, a laywoman provided the funding for her mission. The schools treated indigenous girls the same as French ones, but did not charge them for attendance. Hymns were sung in French and native tongues, while Guyart made efforts to learn the languages of each of the three nations, subsequently producing catechisms, sacred histories, and dictionaries in each of them. Guyart believed the girls would return to their families, not just showing them French manners, but more importantly the new faith of Catholicism. Thus, there was an element of Europeanization, but also missionary intent.

Africa

The effect of colonial interest pre-dating the Council of Trent is also evident in the Portuguese territories in Africa. Portugal could, at least notionally, claim the battle against Islam in the continent as one of its motivating factors, though in reality pecuniary interests, particularly through the slave trade, were its main driver. Admittedly, there were initial missionary attempts following the founding of the Kingdom of the Congo in the first half of the 16th century, but these soon sank under the waves of the slave trade, in service of which merchants and authorities were even willing to sabotage missionary efforts. With little interest in expanding inland, Portuguese priorities were evident in the names given to the coastal regions, such as the Gold Coast and the Slave Coast. Missionary priests were dependent on trade routes to reach the territories; this, combined with a high mortality rate as they tried to acclimatize, meant that there was little interest among Portuguese clergy in serving in the Tropics.

Nevertheless, Jesuits were present from 1560 and trained local Angolans for the priesthood. As was common elsewhere in Jesuit-run seminaries, the candidates were for the secular clergy rather than the Society. There was a strong strain of thought that held European training was best, so only those who had experienced it could become Jesuits. Similar attitudes saw the temporary closure of the seminary for training the local 'mulatto' (those of European and African mixed parentage) population founded at São Tomé in 1571, the bishop in favour of sending candidates to Coimbra in Portugal, though it was reopened in 1595. Slavery, though, was the dominant force; even the Jesuit college opened to train local men for the priesthood at Luanda in Angola was founded on slave money acquired by a Jesuit laybrother before his religious vocation.

However, there were critics of the African slave trade, including the Jesuit Alonso de Sandoval and the Dominicans Fernando Oliveira, Bartolomé de Albornoz, and Tomás de Mercado. They were minority voices but it is notable in 1686 that the Holy See condemned a range of Atlantic slave trade abuses following pressure emanating from descendants of slaves. Lourenço da Silva de Mendouça, a Brazilian 'mulatto' with slave origins in Angola and the Congo, petitioned against 'the diabolic abuse of such slavery', and caught the attention of Propaganda Fide, to whom the pope had referred his complaints. Propaganda promptly contacted the nuncios in Madrid and Lisbon to protest the horrors being committed in the Spanish and Portuguese empires. This was not the only time Propaganda was at odds with the imperialist colonizers. Capuchin missionaries in the Congo soon joined the chorus of criticism. The Capuchins did not merely see slavery as an affront to Catholic principles, but to common humanity, framing it in terms of what we would today regard as universal human rights. The Holy Office pronounced in agreement with Capuchin petitions to effectively condemn the Atlantic slave trade as it was operating. Ultimately, though, crown power was needed to ensure rulings took effect in this Iberian dominated area; simply put, the Portuguese were zealous colonialists intent on slavery and money-making. This meant that there was little real engagement in missionary activity, even to the point where they deliberately worked to its detriment, viewing any African clergy as inevitably inferior. It was not until the 19th century that missionary work in Africa was taken seriously.

Asia

Capuchin loyalty to Propaganda over Iberian imperial interests was also evident in India. Here, Portugal's claims over the direction of the Church, including the appointment of bishops, were frequently in opposition to Roman authority and the independence of papal missions under Propaganda. Initially, activity in India had followed a familiar colonialist template, Portugal setting up a stronghold in Goa by destroying Hindu temples and launching mass conversion campaigns. The numbers of Franciscan and Dominican missionaries gradually grew, while Francis Xavier introduced the Jesuits into the area in the early 1540s. Though Goa and its importance for seafaring trade was the focus of Portuguese interest in Asia, the religious orders looked inland and began working in three principal areas. One focus of activity was the St Thomas Christians of Kerala. Here, the Jesuits sought to 'update' the approach of this ancient Christian community, striving to bring behaviours in line with Tridentine norms such as clerical celibacy. Unsurprisingly, the Keralan communities were often wary of these efforts, fearing they were fronts for Portuguese colonial endeavours. Another area of encounter, though less successful, was the Mughal empire in the north. Despite appearing open to the Jesuit message—not least thanks to the translation of Christian texts into Persian in the 1590s by the great-nephew of Francis Xavier—there were few converts.

Perhaps the most noteworthy initiatives were undertaken in the Tamil areas of southern India, initiated by Francis Xavier in the Gulf of Mannar in 1542. He was followed by the Portuguese Jesuit Henrique Henriques, who laboured there from 1549 to 1600, producing a grammar and several Christian works in Tamil. The *Krista Purana*, which adapted Hindu poetic forms to tell the story from creation to Jesus' time in local languages, was written by an English Jesuit, Thomas Stephens, and first published in 1616. Particularly significant was the approach of the Italian Jesuit Roberto de Nobili, who adopted the dress, diet, and mannerisms of a Hindu holy man, studying Sanskrit and composing moral texts in that language. His form of accommodation saw converts maintain Brahim cultural distinctions, such as markers of the caste system. A Portuguese Jesuit expressed disquiet at this approach, indicating wider tensions around missionary tactics, though de Nobili's methods received the backing of Propaganda and Rome.

Similar tensions were also evident in Goa, where a Christian of the Brahim court, Matheus de Castro, was refused ordination by the bishop. Angered by this decision, he travelled to Rome and visited Propaganda in 1625, where he was subsequently ordained, consecrated as a bishop, and appointed vicar apostolic in the Kingdoms of Bijapur. When he returned to Goa, the Portuguese-appointed civil and ecclesiastical officials refused to recognize his credentials.

Of course, not all missionary behaviour was what we would term enlightened, but the Jesuit college in Goa had 110 students by 1556 comprising eight different Asian-language groups, with students taught in their own tongue in addition to learning in Latin and Portuguese.

The Philippines was in the unusual—some would argue fortunate—position of being a part of the Iberian empire to which the Spanish paid relatively little attention. Generally keeping themselves within the walls of Manila, founded in 1571, the Spanish never colonized the Philippines as they did South America, viewing it principally as a stop-off point on their trade routes. As such, missionary activity took priority over exploitative colonialism; Augustinians arrived in 1575, followed by Franciscans two years later and the appointment of a Dominican as the first bishop in 1579. The bishop sought to bring Dominican friars with him to work in the Philippines but, underlining the dangers of such missionary travel, 18 of the 20 who accompanied him died on the journey.

The religious orders, as well as the Dominican bishop, took on the role of protectors of the native people. They worked to help resist exploitation and slavery, while providing lay education (a Dominican college opened in 1611, becoming a university in 1645) and establishing a printing press, which produced works and grammars in Tagalog. It was not only the Jesuits who took innovative approaches in the missionary arena: the Franciscans here as elsewhere adapted local vernacular songs for the purposes of catechesis. During his brief pontificate (1590–1) Gregory XIV confirmed this accommodationist approach by ordering compensation be paid to any Filipino natives who had been exploited by colonizers and outlawing slavery. In terms of understanding the broader vision of the Catholic Reformation, it is notable that this pope was an admirer of Charles Borromeo and a close acquaintance of Philip Neri. There was still Europeanization in the Philippines—village elites who converted to Catholicism sometimes adopted certain Hispanic characteristics—but, importantly, it integrated more with the local rather than stamping all over it, as was the case in South America.

Revealingly, the two most famous missions in the eastern arena were to lands not colonized by European powers. What Spain sought to do with the sword in South America, the Jesuits sought to do with western science in China. In 1583, the Italian Jesuits Michele Ruggieri and Matteo Ricci landed in China, having spent the previous few years learning the language in Macao. Sporting the shaved heads and clothing of Buddhist monks, they attracted some converts among the lower classes, blending, for example, Buddhist and Ignatian methods of meditation. However, it was Ricci who was to make the real waves in China. Recognizing that the populace revered Confucian philosophers more than Buddhist monks, he cast off the Buddhist attire and instead adopted the manner of a Confucian scholar. He presented Catholicism as the fulfilment of Confucian ethics, as encapsulated by his Chinese work *The True Meaning of the Lord of Heaven*. Ricci also recognized the appeal of European science and mathematics, gaining the favour of the emperor with a mechanical clock and publishing his global *Map of Ten Thousand Empires* with China at its centre.

Soon he was mixing with, and attracting converts from, the Chinese cultural elites. This accommodationist approach meant that in 1630 two Jesuits were appointed to assist with amending the Imperial Calendar; the astronomical achievements of one of them, the German Johann Adam Schall von Bell, were recognized in his appointment as a mandarin. Even during the subsequent ups and downs of the Chinese mission, this scientific knowledge remained at the forefront. For example, the Belgian Jesuit

Ferdinand Verbiest secured the mission's future when he accurately predicted an eclipse around 1671.

None of that is to say the path was smooth in China. It was certainly a dangerous mission field to enter; an estimated third of Jesuits travelling from Lisbon to Macao died en route. Xenophobic suspicion of this 'foreign' religion led to bursts of anti-Christian agitation, which in 1606 resulted in the death by torture of the Chinese Jesuit laybrother Huang Mingshu. As the perception of Catholicism as a foreign influence grew during the later 17th and 18th centuries, the mission came instead to be staffed by local, Chinese clergy. However, a significant blow to the mission was self-inflicted. Dominicans and Franciscans emanating from Spanish territories were highly suspicious of Ricci's practice of accommodation; even some Jesuits rejected it, seeing it as soft-peddling core Christian tenets. This resulted in the Chinese Rites Controversy (see Chapter 7). Accommodation—as espoused by the likes of Francis Xavier and given concrete form by the Jesuit visitor of Asia Alessandro Valignano, in his instructions to missionaries bound for China and Japan—saw the missionary adopt the customs of the host, learn their language, cultivate social elites, and present Catholicism as in keeping with local habits. Propaganda backed this approach rather than, for example, the Europeanizing of South America. Thus, Ricci adopted local customs while simultaneously working to present Catholicism as part of Chinese culture. Such an approach saw, for example, Pope Paul V grant permission for Mass to be said in Chinese.

Francis Xavier never reached his goal of mainland China, dying in 1552 on an island near Macao while waiting for permission to enter the country. However, he had been the first Jesuit to enter Japan in 1549; he subsequently became the model for the Asian missions, having rejected Europeanization in favour of accommodation as the best missionary practice. Once again, the missionaries used Portuguese trading routes and stations as their springboard. By 1559 the Jesuit mission was established at the imperial capital of

Kyoto, with Xavier's approach reinforced in the 1580s by the above-mentioned Jesuit visitor Alessandro Valignano. The latter penned a Japanese-language catechism and recommended that missionaries should, for example, eat Japanese food and recognize cultural manners; graft Catholicism onto Buddhist and Shinto devotions; construct churches in keeping with Japanese architectural styles; and train a local clergy. Success was massive; there were an estimated 300,000 Catholics by 1614, and Christian samurai armies, who marched under the banner of the cross and were served by Jesuit chaplains, were formed.

Two problems soon put an end to what has been termed Japan's Christian century. The first factor was related to internal, national developments. When Xavier arrived, Japan had been made up of different states but, as time passed, the nation was gradually unified, stoking official suspicion of Catholics' allegiance to the pope, whom they viewed as a foreign power. Militant Buddhist hostility towards this 'foreign' religion further exacerbated the situation. The second factor was the arrival of Spanish Franciscans from Manila in 1593. The Jesuits, who accessed the country through Portuguese trade lines, opposed the Franciscans' entry, but the unification of the Spanish and Portuguese crowns meant it became an inevitability. Thus, the Jesuit monopoly on the Japanese mission was broken and the commercial dominance of Portuguese Macao was threatened. Apart from importing to Japan the rivalries between religious orders and European countries, it also fuelled Japanese fears that Christianization meant colonization.

These suspicions first peaked in 1597 when a group of 26 missionaries and Japanese laity were crucified at Nagasaki, including Mexico-City-born Felipe de Jesús and Gonsalo Garcia, who hailed from a mestizo background in India. Dutch Protestant traders further fuelled the fire by spreading anti-Catholic tales and encouraging the persecution to advance their own commercial interests in the region. As a result, all foreign missionaries were expelled from Japan in 1614. Nevertheless, some remained and ministered covertly, and were soon joined by others who secretly entered the country. Official persecution was set in motion and by 1623 all Japanese citizens had to declare their religious allegiance. The authorities quickly realized that the execution of Christians was actually solidifying resistance through a spirit of martyrdom. Thus, they invented a series of tortures; recognizing the power of apostasy, they developed the trial of *e-fumi*, which saw Christians forced to trample on religious imagery as a display of abandoning their faith in the face of threats. Christianity was denounced as foreign. When, for a number of reasons, peasants revolted in 1637–8, the ensuing suppression resulted in 30,000 Christians being put to death.

Old worlds

The Catholic imagination was gripped not only by areas previously untouched by the faith; equally daring—and often more dangerous—was evangelization of places lost to Protestantism right on the edges of Catholic heartlands. The three kingdoms of England, Ireland, and Scotland were officially Protestant by the second half of the 16th century, but the Catholic experience was different in each country. Ireland's populace remained overwhelmingly Catholic, national identity grafted to the faith by missionary Franciscans in opposition to a foreign English occupier, a tactic reminiscent of that adopted by the same order in Bosnia. In contrast, missionary activity in Scotland was always small, as Catholicism wilted before the advance of Protestantism. Both realms saw individuals killed for their faith, but it was England that became synonymous with mission and martyrdom in the early modern Catholic mind. The sacrifice of both clergy and laypeople became a key characteristic of the English Catholic identity; its missionary leaders promoted as much to the public of Catholic Europe in an attempt to win support for their cause (Figure 4).

A. Ob fidem sedi Romanæ seruatam Ioannes forestus ordinis S. Francisci de obseruantia sacerdos uenerandus uiuus suspensus, igneq̃, subsecto cõbustus est, qui accendebatur ligno sacræ Christi statuæ.

B. Secti sunt in quatuor partes post suspendium spirantes doctor Powelus, fetherstonus, Abelus sacerdotes docti, Gardinerus quoq̃, et Larcus Londini: Stoneus item Augustini aruis cantuariæ.

C. tres R^di Abbates ordinis S. Benedicti necantur, et aliquot ipsorum Monachi laqueis collocantur.

4. Niccoló Circignani's *Ecclesiae Anglicanae Trophœa*... (Rome, 1584).

Laws were introduced under Elizabeth I which required the entire population to attend the state Protestant church each Sunday. At first, many Catholics attended to obey the secular law of the land. However, continentally trained missionaries started to arrive in the country after 1574; they promoted non-attendance at the state church, both as a means of demarcating confessional boundaries and stopping the slow defection of Catholics to Protestantism.

This refusal to attend was called recusancy by the authorities and had its roots in the Council of Trent, where a question had been lodged about the English situation. As such, recusancy was a directly Tridentine policy. Following the start of the Jesuit mission to England in 1580, its leaders, Robert Persons and Edmund Campion, effectively argued for freedom of conscience, claiming attendance at religious services was a spiritual rather than secular matter, so the state could not insist upon it. Yet, as Campion himself was fully aware, a country where the head of state and head of the Church was the same person could never accept this division of temporal and spiritual loyalties. As a result, England passed laws decreeing that any person ordained a Catholic priest abroad (the only place where they could be ordained, at one of the exile English colleges established for the purpose) who set foot in England had committed treason, thus effectively outlawing the Catholic priesthood. Any layperson who assisted a missionary priest in any way, knowingly or unknowingly, was also to be sentenced to death.

Those elements characteristic of missionary activity elsewhere were also evident in England. Just as de Nobili sought to convert the elite caste in India, Francis Xavier advocated converting the nation's leadership and aristocracy in Asia, and Matteo Ricci sought to move among the Chinese intellectual and administrative elites, all three believing that this would open up conversion of the whole nation, so the missionaries in England did the same. Although scholars have most frequently applied ideas around accommodation to the Asian mission, such adaptation was also evident in the English arena. For example, missionary priests dressed in secular clothing, even when training on the Continent, in order to avoid detection. They often rode on horses, carried a sword, and used card games as a means to meet people and discuss matters of faith.

Such practices were particularly unusual for Benedictine monks, who arrived on the mission at the start of the 17th century. Unlike monks elsewhere, they did not live in community, instead lodging in the houses of the gentry, under the same roof and in close proximity to women. Indeed, the role of women was vital for the English mission: operating in a grey area of the law, Catholic women exploited the misogyny inherent in English law to be outright recusants and, for example, run safe houses for missionary clergy. The result was that the English state on occasion went to the extreme length of executing women, including Anne Line in London and Margaret Clitherow in York. Still, a question simmered throughout the whole missionary enterprise, particularly in the 17th century: was England by then virgin missionary territory that required the more improvisational approach of the Jesuits, or was it still sufficiently Catholic that the norms of the Tridentine Church, such as bishops and ecclesiastical structures, could operate? The mission subsequently fractured along these lines, the religious orders and the secular clergy espousing different visions of what Catholic Reformation meant. Catholicism remained a proscribed faith in England until 1829.

Another prominent European arena of missionary activity was the Dutch Republic. Fired by anti-Spanish sentiment and the Calvinist faith, the Dutch Revolt had witnessed the martyrdom of Catholic clergy, most notoriously the predominantly Franciscan 19 killed at Gorkum in 1572 for refusing to denounce transubstantiation and papal supremacy. The subsequent formation of the United Provinces of the Netherlands resulted in Catholicism increasingly being viewed as traitorous for its ties not just to the papacy, but particularly to Spain. As in England, Catholics lost a number of their (what we would call) civil rights; it was illegal to have Mass in churches or private houses; Catholics were expected to attend Calvinist preaching; Catholic schools were outlawed. Although Catholics faced fines or confiscation of property for breaking these laws, the persecution was not as intense as in England, partly because 48 per cent of the population remained Catholic by 1648. Also unlike England, Rome did not wait long to create some sort of ecclesiastical oversight of the area, with the appointment of the Jesuit Sasbout Vosmeer as vicar apostolic with responsibility for the Dutch mission. From his base in the southern Netherlands, Vosmeer largely appointed secular clergy for the mission from exile colleges formed for that very purpose, as was the tactic for the English, Irish, and Scottish missions. He deliberately avoided utilizing too many Jesuits due to their Spanish connections, which could inflame local authorities. Mass was said in discreet chapels like one in an attic in Amsterdam, Vosmeer turning to lay leadership of the mission, securing permission from Rome to create a para-diaconate who could organize religious services without a priest, plus read litanies, prayers, and sermons in the vernacular, offering another example of accommodation and adaptation within the Catholic Reformation.

As in England, the role of women was again vital; this church was effectively run by celibate holy women, known as *kloppen*, who organized and cared for Mass stations, let people know service times, read the lessons at Mass, potentially arranged for music during the liturgies, visited the sick, taught children, and raised poor relief. By 1700, there were roughly 5,000 *kloppen* pioneering a lay-led church that placed a heavy emphasis on personal religious commitment. Nevertheless, there were still disagreements between clerical groups over Tridentine mission tactics; at the hard edges of the Catholic Reformation, they were literally arguing over potentially life and death matters.

Plurality of approaches

Due to the size of their empires, Spain and Portugal initially dominated the global missionary field, but as the 17th century progressed, France became increasingly active. The Paris Foreign Missions Society (Société des Missions Étrangères de Paris) was founded in 1659 with the help of the French Jesuit Alexandre de

Rhodes. He wrote about his own missionary experiences in Vietnam for a French audience, as well as studying the Vietnamese language, penning the *Ngắm Mùa Chay*, a reflection on the Passion in Vietnamese to help locals pray during Lent. Moreover, missionaries of different nationalities were active in numerous other countries not mentioned above, such as Borneo, Cambodia, and Burma. The Church truly went global in the Catholic Reformation.

Events in South America tend to dominate modern popular consciousness when this period is mentioned, but how much of what went on there was actually indicative of the Catholic Reformation? After all, Iberian activity in these arenas often pre-dated the Council of Trent; behaviour in South America may actually be an outlier. Certainly, Propaganda Fide, that totem of Catholic Reformation institutional expression, seemed to think differently, and there were tensions with Iberian colonialist interests. As well as the examples given earlier, there were other critics. For example, two Capuchins, the Spanish Francisco de Jaca and the Frenchman Épiphanie de Moirans, were both excommunicated by the Iberian-appointed bishop in Havana, Cuba, in 1681 for preaching that slaves should be freed by their owners and paid for their labours. They refused to grant absolution to any who did not promise to do this. Yet Iberian rights over the Church, including episcopal appointments, meant that the political allegiance of 'yes men' could win out against the prophetic voices raised by members of religious orders and sometimes even Rome itself. Indeed, the early proponents of Catholic reform had railed against worldly and secular entanglement, desiring to purge it from the Church. Here, then, is one of the hallmarks of the Catholic Reformation, the tension between the local and the centres. This might explain why the mission to Asia—rather than the older, colonially compromised one to South America—gripped the imagination of Catholic Europe. There might even be a case for arguing that the missionary enterprise of the Catholic Reformation truly began in 1580, the year when missionaries gained permission to enter China, Valignano launched his programme for accommodated mission in Japan, and the Jesuits arrived in England.

Without question, there were different visions of the Catholic Reformation. Apart from the distinctly Iberian approach, clashes were witnessed in all the missionary arenas, often between religious orders and bishops over jurisdictional claims, but also between different orders. At root, almost all these disputes boiled down to one question: what should Tridentine Catholicism look like? Ultimately, plurality, not uniformity, was the hallmark of Catholic Reformation missionary activity.

Chapter 5
Catholic living

Whether a person was in Europe, Asia, Africa, or the Americas, Catholic life was deeply affected by the global missionary enterprise outlined in the previous chapter. In Japan, a Jesuit likened Catholic suffering to the persecution in England, while in 1622 the English-language *The Theater of Iaponia's Constancy* was published, meaning two Catholic missions referenced each other's persecution across thousands of miles. Equally, books detailing the fates of the English martyrs appear to have been circulated in the Americas, while in Milan, Charles Borromeo, a fervent benefactor of the English mission, also preached on the evangelization of the Far East. In the final years of the 16th century, Japanese converts were brought to Italy by the Jesuits. They created a sensation; received with pomp at Rome and Milan, the visit mobilized popular support for the Asian mission. Moreover, Matteo Ricci's journals were published in Europe, promoting the Chinese mission and again capturing the imagination of Catholic Europe. Drawn from across the global Catholic Reformation, these elements helped to shape the life of individual Catholics, which is the focus of this chapter.

Relics and sanctity

Material reminders of heroic martyrs from across the globe were a mainstay of Tridentine Catholic life. Towards the end of the

Council of Trent, the delegates had pronounced in favour of the veneration of relics of holy people, including martyrs. Shortly after, in 1578, the catacombs were discovered in Rome and instantly interpreted as a sign of the Church's unbroken continuity from the early Roman martyrs. It was not hard to make the case that those killed for their faith in antiquity had their contemporary successors in places like England. Apart from underlining the relationship between the Church's past and present, this discovery combined with contemporary mission activity to create an intense desire for relics. As William Allen, the first leader of England's Catholic mission, wrote: 'the Catholics, of Italy, Spain, France, and namely (which is less to be marveled at) of England, more than the weight in gold would be given, and is offered for any piece of their [English martyrs'] relics, either of their bodies, hair, bones, or garments, yes or any thing that hath any spot or stain of their innocent and sacred blood'.

Simply put, relics were a defining feature of lived Catholicism in the early modern period, an important focus of veneration and a material link to heaven, common to both the peripheries and the centres of Catholic Reformation. For example, a relic of Francis Xavier, that symbol of global mission, was originally destined for Japan but was stalled at Macau due to the ongoing persecution; meanwhile, his right arm was transported to Rome and displayed at the Jesuits' principal church, the Gesù. As well as relics being rescued from desecration in areas of Protestant ascendancy—such as those of St Benno smuggled from Meissen to Munich's Catholic cathedral, or St Norbert's from Magdeburg to Prague—they were also harnessed in efforts to re-Catholicize territories previously 'lost' to Protestantism. In places like the Upper Palatinate, Catholicism's revival following a period of Protestant ascendancy was marked by the return of relics in lavish ceremonies. This emphasis upon relics was only strengthened by the Tridentine command that all altars should contain a saint's relic, thus encouraging the spread of catacomb relics from Rome outwards. This instruction also created another spiritual bond across the globe.

The process of creating saints became a much more bureaucratic affair during the Catholic Reformation. Trent had reasserted the role of saints as intercessors in heaven in the face of Protestant attack, but had still taken aim at superstitions that had accrued around them, as well as money-making schemes attached to particular devotions. The more fantastical local saints' cults were jettisoned in favour of a centralized, scientific approach to the investigation of miracles as signs of sanctity. The Congregation of Rites was established in 1588 as part of a decades-long reform effort in this area, primarily to deal with liturgy, but also the canonization process. Over six decades it introduced set procedures for investigating a person's sanctity, such as gathering witness statements and reaffirming that only the papacy could officially recognize someone as a saint.

These tighter processes meant a rapid decline in the frequency of canonizations—only 27 men and women who lived between 1540 and 1770 were declared saints in that same period. Those who were officially recognized as saints were congruent with the main thrusts of the Catholic Reformation, such as the embodiment of the Tridentine bishop Charles Borromeo. The New World expansion of the Catholic Reformation was reflected in the Dominican nun Rose of Lima—who in 1671 became the first canonized saint to be born in the Americas—the fabled global missioner Francis Xavier, and the Franciscan Francisco Solano, who worked with the Indians of Peru. Perhaps most notable were the number of founders of reform religious orders, including those of the Jesuits, the Oratorians, the Somaschi, the Theatines, the Camillians, and the Visitandines.

In addition to these new orders, those who led reform of older ones were also recognized as saints, most notably Teresa of Avila of the Discalced Carmelites, an individual whose spirituality was initially considered controversial (a common theme across several reforming figures), but who became hugely influential, to the point where the University of Salamanca granted her a title during her lifetime. Veneration of older saints of course continued, plus for all that these new, exemplary figures of the Catholic Reformation were intended as global inspiration, they were real people connected to specific places. Their followings—known as cults—came from a locality and, though it was Rome that might make saints official, it was the laity who engaged with the devotions, and the role of local promoters to secure that official stamp of approbation. As such, local saints helped forge regional Catholic identities. For example, though he may have had wider renown, Francis Xavier was held in particular reverence in Asia. In 1603, the Dutch priest William Estius published a history of the Gorkum martyrs, *Historia Martyrum Gorcomiensium*. By 1621, the Congregation of Rites had approved their cult and they were subsequently beatified in 1675. It is noteworthy that Estius also translated a life of the English Jesuit martyr Edmund Campion. In short, there was room for both the local and the universal within the Catholic Reformation.

Fighting a spiritual war

In their role as heavenly intercessors, the saints were part of what was termed the Church Triumphant. Although nowadays the terms are frequently misapplied, the other two categories into which all Catholics fell were the Church Militant and the Church Suffering. The term Church Militant had nothing to do with secular warfare, but expressed the view that Catholics lived as soldiers of Christ fighting against sin and the devil. The Church Suffering were those souls who were in purgatory; they were suffering because they knew they would reach heaven, but it was a delayed pleasure while their souls were cleansed. The Church Triumphant were those souls that had made it to heaven. Given the backgrounds of several of the key reforming figures in Tridentine Catholicism, the military-style terminology is of note, but particularly important for understanding the Catholic Reformation is that, again, the onus was placed on the individual. Every Catholic was engaged in their own battle against sin.

The parish church was the main site for training in this warfare. The Council of Trent had emphasized the importance of the parish within the diocese, and had placed great weight on raising the standard of parish clergy. Priests, as well as bishops, were to preach regularly to the laity. The emphasis on preaching was just as characteristic of Catholic reformers as Protestant, with the new religious orders particularly devoted to it, hence the missionary appetite for local languages. In an effort to raise the level of preaching quickly, sermon texts were provided for the parish clergy, such as the three volumes of *Promptuarium Catholicum* published between 1589 and 1594. It was written by the Englishman Thomas Stapleton, based in exile at Leuven University, underlining the circular relationship between centres and peripheries in the Catholic Reformation. The volumes provided sermon texts for each Sunday, all major church feasts, and the weekdays of Lent, and combined biblical scholarship, pastoral intent, and polemical criticism of Protestant biblical interpretations. The work was hugely influential in the Catholic reform of parishes in early modern Europe and by 1598 there had been 57 printings of the various volumes across the printing capitals of the Continent. But even within preaching, there were different interpretations of how best to achieve total Catholic Reformation. Charles Borromeo was a great advocate of preaching in a simple, catechetical, edifying style to reach all levels of society, including the less educated. In contrast, the Jesuits favoured a classical oration style grounded in theology and philosophy, very much aimed at a cultured audience. Thus, in a city, the laity had different options and could choose to attend a church they favoured, very often based on the style of preaching to be found there.

Parish missions, particularly in rural locations, were another device aimed at galvanizing and renewing Catholic faith. Various branches of the Franciscans, particularly the Capuchins, as well as dedicated orders like Vincent de Paul's Lazarists, were committed to missions aimed at the peasantry. Frequently as dramatic as they were catechetical, these missions disrupted the routine cycle of parish life and employed similar methods wherever they took place from South America to Europe. Over eight days the missionaries would preach, catechize, organize processions and penitential exercises, and exhort the people to confession and communion. Embodying the spirt of Catholic Reformation, these local events were inspired by the exact same missionary impulse all over the globe.

Sacramental life cycle

The life cycle of Catholics was punctuated by the sacraments of the Church. The Council of Trent had reaffirmed the traditional seven sacraments in the face of Protestant critique and even repudiation, and Catholic reformers placed a matching emphasis on individual interior reform and commitment. Three principal methods were deployed to aid this: regular parish visitations by the bishop, the gathering of information, and education. The last saw the steady development of catechisms, the process given real impetus by the German-language catechism of 1555 by the Dutch Jesuit Peter Canisius, which played a significant role in halting the march of Protestantism in Germany, and the Roman catechism of 1566, to which Charles Borromeo was a significant contributor. As outlined earlier, vernacular catechisms became a significant tool of Catholic reform.

The first sacrament encountered by all Catholics was baptism. The Catholic Reformation sought to remove questionable practices around this sacrament that had built up in the medieval period. Speedy baptism with a limit of two godparents became the norm, moving away from elaborate kinship networking that could delay the ceremony (a problem in an era of high infant mortality). The Tridentine catechism recommended naming children after saints and the laity seemed to agree. The Council of Trent also introduced the notion of the priest as record keeper, requiring that all parishes maintain registers of baptism and marriage. Though baptism was generally a sacrament performed on newborns, questions arose over adult baptism in the global missionary arena, particularly around the mass baptisms performed in South America, which were scorned by a number of Catholic reformers who advocated the need for proper individual instruction. Here again, despite there being a norm, circumstances often required flexibility.

The two most frequently encountered sacraments were those of confession and communion. Trent had reaffirmed Catholic belief in transubstantiation; that is, that the wafer and the wine became the body and blood of the risen Christ at the moment of consecration during the Mass. In contrast to Protestantism, lay Catholics only received communion under one kind; the chalice containing the Precious Blood was reserved for the priest. Pope Pius IV had briefly allowed the chalice to be taken by the laity in central Europe after lobbying by the Holy Roman Emperor, but it was withdrawn 20 years later, in 1584, as it caused confusion, the taking of 'the cup' being associated with Protestantism in people's minds.

The period of Catholic reform prompted better catechesis and instruction before somebody received communion for the first time. This in turn led to the start of group First Communion Masses, children who had been instructed as a class making it together. Catholic belief was that a person could only receive communion if they had been to confession and had their sins forgiven, meaning that they were in a state of grace. The Catholic Reformation saw the widespread introduction of the confessional, with Charles Borromeo a major supporter. At its most basic level, the priest sat behind a grille, on the other side of which a penitent would kneel. Some historians have said this was an effort by the Church to exert power and control, but the goal can be seen as the same as reform more generally; it encouraged individual, private examination of one's conscience, the grille supposedly creating anonymity as the priest took on the Gospel injunction from Jesus to 'loose and bind on earth', acting as a conduit to God through which the confessed sins and subsequent forgiveness flowed. Contact with the priest thus became more regular in this new sacramental set-up, the intention being that he could console and guide the individual layperson. Regular confession and communion were advocated, though many still held to the traditional minimal adherence of confession during Holy Week in preparation for Easter communion. It was this repeated cycle of confession and communion that people experienced through most of their lives.

The Catholic Reformation also saw a re-engagement with the sacrament of confirmation. The catechism of the Council of Trent (also known as the Roman catechism) used the language of the Church Militant waging battle against sin: 'In Baptism man is enlisted into the service, in Confirmation he is equipped for battle; at the baptismal font the Holy Ghost imparts fullness to accomplish innocence, but in Confirmation he ministers perfection to grace ... Confirmation arms and makes ready for conflicts.' Nevertheless, confirmation remained the poor relation of the sacraments, not least because it could only be administered by bishops, who were often in short supply in many missionary fields.

Marriage was another sacrament that went through a process of reform. Prior to Trent, so-called clandestine marriages were allowed, which judged a verbal contract between a man and a woman as sufficient. Perhaps unsurprisingly, this led to much dispute, with a number of cases of men reneging on their promise after consummation, resulting in pregnancy and charges of seduction. Trent insisted that marriage was a public ceremony, decreeing that it should occur in the church with the vows witnessed by a minimum of three people, one of these being a priest. Those at the council were also concerned about potential parental pressure so insisted on the free consent of the couple to marry, which the priest was charged with upholding. This could be interpreted as ecclesiastical control being exerted, priestly authority trumping kinship interests, but at the same time these reforms sought to halt abuses around marriage that particularly harmed women. This was a notable effort that saw the Catholic Reformation start to pay serious attention to the obligations of a husband towards his wife, based on the equality conferred by baptism.

The Catholic attitude towards holy orders emphasized formation, as well as free choice, particularly where women religious were concerned. The vows of women religious were similar to those of marriage, in that the nuns became brides of Christ, their profession gowns looking like early modern wedding dresses. It was also decreed that no girl under the age of 16 could make final profession vows. Women religious followed a set path of formation like men entering the clergy, with defined stages on the path towards the sacrament of Holy Orders. Like nuns, a minimum age for priestly ordination was set, this time 24. As a demarcation from Protestantism, Catholicism insisted upon priestly celibacy and sought to eliminate concubinage. This took longer to implement in rural areas, particularly in Italy, but was increasingly the case with the new cadre of Tridentine priest. The overall effect of such reforms was a notable improvement in the quality of parish clergy during the 17th century.

The final sacrament in the life cycle of all Catholics was extreme unction, more popularly known as the last rites. This involved a priest attending the deathbed to recite prayers and anoint the body of the dying, preparing their soul for the next stage. Particular emphasis came to be placed on a good death, especially a thorough deathbed confession.

The overarching purpose of the sacramental life cycle was to get a person to heaven. Anybody who made it into heaven was a saint;

only a small number of people were officially declared saints by the Church, but the real number of those in heaven was known only to God. The souls of the few officially recognized as saints may have gone straight to heaven, as was believed the case with martyrs, but the best hope for the vast majority was to reach purgatory. Purgatory can best be understood as God's waiting room, a place where souls would be purified in readiness for the beatific vision. Confessed sins may have been forgiven during a person's life, but purgatory saw the cleansing of any happy memory of them: for example, someone may have drunk excessively and been absolved of that sin, but they may still have enjoyed a happy memory of it. The purported pains and agonies of the souls in purgatory makes people think of the medieval visions of fire and torture. Though such imagery was still utilized, a more accurate understanding is that the agony was knowing one would be with God, but having to wait for it. That is why those on earth could pray for the souls in purgatory, including their loved ones, in an effort to help them reach heaven more quickly. The laity could also pray for the intercession of souls already in heaven. Both those in purgatory and heaven could also pray for those still living, creating a cosmic dimension to the Catholic life cycle. The only ones cut off were those souls who went to hell, unrepentant of their mortal sins, hence the Catholic reformers' advocation of frequent confession.

Women played a major role within this sacramental life cycle. In charge of the domestic space, they set the religious atmosphere of the house, holding a key position in the catechesis of children. For this reason the education of girls (increasingly provided by women religious) played a vital role in the Catholic Reformation, as these girls were the Catholic mothers of the future. In short, women were fundamental to catechesis, the *kloppen* in the Dutch Republic an extreme example of a more widespread phenomenon. In places like Münster and Bavaria in Germany, lay women known as the *Lichtmütter* shaped parish life, helping to maintain churches and collect alms. In Ireland, the short-lived group of women known as *Mná Bochta* (Poor Women) were engaged in active charitable ministry, particularly to prostitutes, an initiative common in the Catholic Reformation.

Living the devotional life

This leads to the question of how the devotional life was actually lived. Confraternities were extremely popular with the laity. They had developed in late medieval Christianity and were associations of laypeople formed in dedication to particular saints around people's jobs, crafts, or locality. They were both religious and social, with common devotional practices and often an element of caring for the sick and the poor. In that sense, they anticipated the Catholic Reformation's more active role in charitable work; for example, the Bethlehemite order founded in the 1650s in Guatemala City to provide health care to the poor had its roots in a confraternity. Importantly, confraternities were voluntary lay associations. Ecclesiastical authorities supported the increase in such lay devotions, but sought to rein in the festal excesses indulged in by some. This can be interpreted as increased clerical control, but that underplays the laity's agency; for example, in Florence, the confraternity of Santa Maria del Bigallo gave up their traditional feasts, leaving to the clergy what belonged in the spiritual sphere while lobbying the secular for a role in welfare provision for the poor. Confraternities usually had their own chapel or altar in the local church, dedicating themselves to collective devotional exercises, mutual support and assistance, and philanthropy. Prayers for deceased members were a fundamental aspect of this mutual support. Indeed, many confraternities were associated with events around death and judgement, such as that dedicated to St Barbara in Antwerp, which prayed for a holy death. Some were open to both men and women, and confraternities assisted parish priests in the Church's mission in the locality. Many were associated with religious orders, which, as elsewhere, could cause friction with parish clergy, another manifestation of that unresolved tension between the orders and diocesan structures at the heart of the Catholic Reformation.

Confraternities existed right across the Catholic world. For example, those dedicated to the Blessed Sacrament or the Rosary were particularly popular among the indigenous people of what is now Mexico. Underlining the voluntary nature of confraternities and the level of lay agency involved, the Capuchin mission to Congo and Angola saw the establishment in Luanda of the Confraternity of the Holy Rosary, membership of which was for the Black population and slaves. In 1658, the confraternity petitioned Rome for protection against colonialist would-be enslavers because 'in the service of God we must all be equal'. In Bahia in Brazil, a confraternity with the same dedication was limited to the Black population of Angolan descent, and subsequently became an early modern mouthpiece for their rights.

Lourenço da Silva de Mendouça came from this environment. He was able to protest to Propaganda against slavery partly because he had been appointed procurator of the Confraternity of Our Lady Star of the Negroes in Madrid in 1682, which meant he could establish branches anywhere. This confraternity, strong in Brazil and parts of Africa, raised funds to help support the sick or those in prison. By the late 17th century, Black confraternities were well established in Brazil and Portugal, while the first such confraternity in Spain had been founded at Cadiz in 1593. Lay religious devotion was a fundamental of Catholic reformers and, in the example of Black confraternities, the unpredictable path of reform is again evident, their existence clearly a challenge to some Iberian attitudes.

The regular church year was given extra spice by feast days. The liturgical calendar was streamlined over several decades, but major universal feasts, as well as local saints' days, remained. The feast of Corpus Christi, with its focus on the consecrated host as the body of Christ, became even more prominent as a counter to

Protestant beliefs. The feast day involved the priest, holding aloft a monstrance containing the consecrated host, leading a procession involving most of the populace through the local streets, literally bringing God to the town. Devotion to the real presence was also expressed through what was known as the *Quarant'Ore*. For 40 hours, the consecrated host was displayed for veneration in the church, a practice praised by the likes of Charles Borromeo and Philip Neri and advocated by Francis de Sales.

Pilgrimage was another area of Catholic devotional life given new impetus after Protestant critique. Pilgrimages continued across the Catholic world, including in territories under Protestant persecution, such as to St Patrick's Purgatory at Lough Derg in Ireland. Loreto was a major devotional site near Ancona in Italy; the Holy House in which Mary had been told by the angel Gabriel that she was pregnant with Jesus was believed to have been transported there. Key Catholic Reformation figures such as Francis Xavier, Charles Borromeo, and Francis de Sales were among the pilgrims who trooped to the site. Devotion to Our Lady of Loreto grew to such an extent that replicas of the Holy House were made, including in North and South America. The Habsburgs even constructed a copy in Vienna, under the custodianship of the Augustinians.

This touches on another major devotional movement in Tridentine Catholicism. The role of the Virgin Mary as heavenly intercessor had been attacked by Protestant reformers, but was revitalized during the Catholic Reformation. The vigour of devotions surrounding the Virgin cannot be underestimated, ranging from the growing popularity of the ringing of the angelus bell in the 17th century to confraternities of the Holy Rosary promoted by the Dominicans and Jesuits. Marian sodalities blossomed. Initially founded for students at Jesuit colleges—the first originated at the Roman College in 1563—sodality members met for communal prayer, observed the feast days relating to Mary, and regularly received holy communion. They soon spread throughout urban society, membership made up of a new Tridentine elite, both in the secular and ecclesiastical spheres. Crossing all strata of society, the movement was particularly popular in Flanders and Lorraine, as well as parts of Germany and Italy. In contrast to the lack of a devotional female focus in Protestantism, Maximilian of Bavaria declared Mary the *Generalissima* of the Catholic armies at the battle of White Mountain. Pope Pius V had previously encouraged the recitation of the Rosary before the battle of Lepanto in 1572 against the Turkish navy. In recognition of her role in the victory, he established the feast of Our Lady of Victory, subsequently changed to Our Lady of the Rosary, on 7 October.

Devotion to the Virgin was a global phenomenon, with significant cults present in South America (Figure 5). In December 1531, in what is modern-day Mexico, the indigenous peasant Juan Diego received a series of visions of the Virgin, resulting in the cult of Our Lady of Guadalupe. Elsewhere, the cult of the Virgin of Copacabana in modern-day Bolivia was spurred on by Francisco Tito Yupanqui, a sculptor descended from the Quechua people. Just as Tridentine Catholicism could become a tool of resistance even against those who claimed to be its architects, so too could the Virgin be co-opted: an image known as the Virgin of the Carmine inspired the poor of Naples in the Masaniello revolt against harsh Spanish taxes on food in 1647.

Innovative theology versus policing the boundaries

Mary was also the focus of a particular theological development within the Catholic Reformation. There was a great deal of creativity in Catholic theology in the period. Growing support for declaring the Immaculate Conception of Mary is a case in point. The Immaculate Conception is about the birth of Mary and the belief that, unlike all humankind apart from Jesus, Mary was free from original sin (i.e. the inherited sinfulness from Adam and Eve's 'original sin' in the Garden of Eden), from the moment of conception in her mother's womb. Thus, Mary was fit to carry

5. *Virgin of Carmel Saving Souls in Purgatory* (**Peruvian, late 17th century**).

Jesus as wholly God and wholly man. Theologians had been making this case since the 12th century and, notably, Trent never ruled on the matter. However, when pronouncing on the universality of original sin, the council fathers did declare, 'that it is not its intentions to include in this decree, which deals with original sin, the blessed and immaculate Virgin Mary, the mother of God'. This was tantamount to recognizing the groundswell of opinion towards confirming the Immaculate Conception, and it only grew as the Catholic Reformation progressed. Philip IV of Spain was a great promoter of the cult of the Immaculate Conception throughout the Iberian world, though perhaps the greatest standard bearers of this position came from the peripheries. At their exile colleges in Leuven and Rome, the Irish Franciscans under the leadership of Luke Wadding championed this theological opinion. Their Aula Maxima at St Isidore's in Rome was decorated to recognize Irish Franciscan promotion of the doctrine, while their college founded in Prague was named in honour of the Immaculate Conception. Theological speculation was not confined to the Immaculate Conception; for example, the Spanish Dominican Francisco de Vitoria's Salamanca School—whose adherents included Domingo de Soto, OP and Francisco Suárez, SJ—reconsidered natural law as a challenge to brutal colonialism in South America.

Naturally, such theologizing could lead to disagreements. Different schools of theology came to dominate specific religious orders, resulting in the Dominicans regularly sparring with the Jesuits. The other side to such debates and theological speculation was the policing of confessional boundaries, an issue brought into even sharper focus by the breakaway of various shades of Protestantism. Perhaps the most notorious element of coercion associated with the Catholic Reformation is the Inquisition. For all that it still grips popular imagination, the geographic reach of the Inquisition was markedly limited. It was a particularly Iberian phenomenon rather than a hallmark of global Catholic reform.

The exception was the Roman Inquisition, which had been reactivated in 1542 in response to the perceived threat of Protestant advance. It was an ecclesiastical court for the discovery of heresy. Famously and shockingly to modern minds, it could use force to bring about the repentance of individuals and to warn others about embracing similar beliefs. Though paradoxical, this is because the Inquisition was pastoral in intent and the Church believed itself to have a responsibility for the salvation of the souls of all the baptized. As such, all punishments were supposed to deter would-be heretics and provoke repentance. To begin with, it was preoccupied with Protestant heresy, though the scope did expand, with foreigners a regular focus of suspicion. The Roman Inquisition was characterized by its adherence to careful legal procedures, its refusal to accept anonymous denunciations, the requirement of two witnesses to corroborate allegations, and the guarantee of a defence lawyer for the accused, while most of the sentences were light. Despite the Roman Inquisition's operational inefficiencies and inconsistencies in how its jurisdiction was enforced, people still practised self-censorship to avoid catching its attention, policing their behaviours accordingly.

No mitigating features existed for the Iberian inquisitions, which were a tool of the monarchy. The Spanish Inquisition was established in 1478 and, as indicated in Chapter 3, was fuelled by paranoia about the enemy within, particularly *conversos* and *moriscos*. It and the Portuguese Inquisition—which was established in 1536, similarly under royal control—operated entirely independently from Rome. Both were organized by a general office fed into by several regional ones. By the late 17th century, there were 21 tribunals in Spanish territories, including at Lima and Mexico City, feeding into a central body whose members were appointed by the Spanish crown as part of royal government. In the case of Portugal, the Inquisition of Lisbon had responsibility for Brazil and the Atlantic Islands, while that of Goa looked after Portuguese colonies in the global East. Even in South America, the Iberian Inquisition was drunk on the same preoccupations, including *conversos* and the secret enemy within. The Spanish Inquisition relied on denunciations and was staffed by clerics, with the Dominican Order the self-styled protectors of Catholic orthodoxy.

Condemnations and reconciliations were major public events. If necessary, civic authorities carried out the punishments for crimes that soon included not just heresy, but misdemeanours like sexual crimes, underlining the secular tie-up of political and religious concerns in the Iberian world. The Spanish Inquisition was an unquestionably oppressive force, making people's self-censorship even more necessary to avoid its reach. It was a phenomenon peculiar to Spain and its territories; France and other countries did not permit an inquisition to function. Moreover, the Spanish passion for it drew criticism elsewhere, and places such as Venice greatly restricted the Inquisition's power. Equally, its most brutal campaigns against *conversos* and *moriscos* pre-dated the Catholic Reformation.

This is an important point because the Inquisition notoriously harassed figures and movements now considered shining beacons of the Catholic Reformation. When Carafa was head of the Roman Inquisition, it interested itself in the Barnabites and the female leader of the closely associated Angelics. In 1559, the Spanish Inquisition arrested the newly appointed Dominican archbishop of Toledo, Bartolomé Carranza. It was suspicious of his activities in Protestant-riddled countries and his production of a Spanish-language catechism, despite it having been backed by those gathered at the Council of Trent. Even the pope lobbied for his release. The spiritual autobiography composed by Teresa of Avila at the behest of her confessor in 1565 was investigated by the Spanish Inquisition and only published in 1588, six years after her death. Standard bearers of the global Catholic Reformation such as the Capuchins aroused much suspicion at the Inquisition, while attempts were made to reform the Jesuits to look more like a traditional religious order. In Peru, the Inquisition investigated the followers of Rose of Lima. As witnessed by Teresa of Avila's experience, the Dominican-packed Spanish Inquisition was particularly suspicious of mysticism and the Jesuits' founder Ignatius of Loyola was questioned on several occasions. Even Catholics from Ireland or England, emblems of the persecuted global Church, often fell under suspicion after fleeing to Spain as refugees because they hailed from officially Protestant states. In other words, with its strong secular ties, the Inquisition was sometimes more an enemy, rather than a tool, of the Catholic Reformation.

Closely linked to the Inquisition was the Index. The first Roman Index of prohibited books was published in 1559 under Paul IV, who had previously headed the Inquisition. Underlining the different interpretations of how to pursue Catholic reform, its severity drew sharp criticism from prominent figures such as the Dutch Jesuit Peter Canisius—whose German-language catechism did so much to halt the march of Protestantism in Germany—and the Spaniard Diego Laínez, who had succeeded Ignatius of Loyola as superior general of the Jesuits. Partly due to this reaction, the Council of Trent attempted to ameliorate the situation, placing the authority of censorship with bishops, but the Roman Index was fully revived by Pope Pius V, who established the Congregation of the Index in 1571. By the end of the 16th century, the Roman Index had prohibited just over 2,000 books. In the Iberian world, the Inquisition published lists of prohibited books, but after 1600 followed the Roman lead. The Index's main focus was heretical books written by Protestants, but it also came to encompass writings that were judged to undermine good morals or dealt with matters of the occult. Books were examined and sometimes reading could be permitted with certain parts expurgated by the censor.

The Inquisition also became sensitive to perceived criticisms of orthodox Catholic teaching. This helps explain why the works of Erasmus remained banned, but the concern stretched to, for example, the Venetian Servite Paolo Sarpi's history of the Council of Trent that criticized the politicking of the papal curia. Banned books were held in a locked part of Catholic libraries often nicknamed 'Hell'; special permission from either a censor or bishop was required to read a text from this section. This hints, though, at a problem around the question of authority within the Catholic Reformation: did the final say on censorship rest with the Inquisition, the Congregation of the Index, or with the local bishop? Certainly, with the Inquisition strong in Rome and the Iberian world, the Index carried more weight there than in northern Europe or the missionary arenas. In those places, monitoring books was the responsibility of bishops or universities, such as the Sorbonne or Leuven. This meant the policing of the Index was not as tight as is often imagined, with significant geographical variations. Licences to read prohibited books were not uncommon and the heads of religious orders were often given the right to extend unlimited licences to their members.

Despite all this, the intent behind the Inquisition and the Index was pastoral. In early modern Europe, heresy was considered a poison that seeped into the bodies politic and social; it only took a drop to pollute and corrupt an individual. In some ways the Catholic Reformation was too successful at creating a sense of horror around the idea of heresy silently infecting society and corrupting all it touched. The Inquisition relied on at least some popular support in order to garner information about cases, suggesting contemporaries shared concerns over religious dissent and immorality. Nevertheless, the Inquisition and Index have been held up as proof that the Catholic Reformation was all about reaction to Protestant advance. Both came to dominate the Protestant imagination as signs of Catholic repression from which they believed themselves freed.

Though devastating for those caught up in their processes, the impact of the Inquisition and the Index was geographically limited, and varied in scope, as well as being the focus of some criticism from within Catholicism. They show the two impulses at work within the Catholic Reformation. One impetus, and the driving one, was to inspire personal spiritual reform and renewal; the other sought to enforce conformity, for example utilizing parish registers of attendance and certificates to say that a person had fulfilled their minimal confession and communion obligations. Notably, such practices also existed in confessionalized Protestant states like England. In other words, Catholic reform looked very different in those countries where church institutions worked as part of the apparatus of state, ecclesiastical structures becoming compliant with secular needs in places like the Iberian world.

Chapter 6
Sensing and thinking Catholicism

At the heart of the Catholic life reformers sought to establish was the Mass. The central moment of the Mass was the consecration, when the wafer and the wine became the body and blood of Christ. Protestantism had rejected this idea, seeing it instead as a commemoration of Christ's words at the Last Supper. For them, the crucifixion and resurrection were historic, one-off events to be memorialized. It was here, with its re-emphasis on the Real Presence of Christ in the eucharist, that Catholic reformers distinguished their theology from that of the Protestants. At every Catholic Mass, Christ's sacrifice was relived and the altar was the calvary on which the drama was played out. At the moment of consecration, when the priest raised the host above his head, heaven and earth were momentarily joined in union, the altar surrounded by the saints in heaven.

To affirm and convey this belief, the Catholic Reformation harnessed all the senses. Eschewing the plain and even sombre surroundings of Protestantism at its most iconoclastic, and its reliance on the written and spoken word for religious engagement, the Catholic Mass at its highest became a sensory overload designed to offer the laity a glimpse of heaven. The richly decorated church building, adorned with statues and paintings and lit by candles, was filled with the smell of incense. Through the clouds of incense could be

6. Chasuble with spangles (probably Italy, late 17th century).

glimpsed the priest at the altar, facing the tabernacle atop it, dressed in rich vestments—sometimes stitched with spangles (Figure 6), catching the candlelight through the mist—as music rang out, sometimes sung by nuns hidden from public view, evoking a choir of angels. No lay Catholic experiencing this could help but appreciate that something special was happening at the Mass. Clearly, not every Mass was celebrated this lavishly, but it underscores the idea that the Catholic Reformation harnessed the sensory whether through art, architecture, or music. Vitally, it also sought to engage the mind and intellect. In short, the Catholic Reformation wanted every part of a person to be devoted to Christ. To achieve this, it touched on all aspects of life.

Architecture and art

Catholic Reformation theology was conveyed in the visual and the material, even to the tiniest detail. For example, whereas Protestant churches removed the figure of Christ from crosses to underline their belief that Jesus had died and risen once, Catholicism exalted the crucifix, keeping the figure of Christ firmly on the cross. Monstrances—used to display the consecrated host in Corpus Christi processions, benediction, or eucharistic adoration—frequently depicted sun rays bursting out from the host, underlining the belief of Christ in the eucharist as the centre of life. A particularly vivid example designed by Johannes Zeckl in Augsburg in 1705 (Figure 7) portrays the Last Supper in silverwork. All the apostles look towards the centre of the table, but there is no carving of Jesus; instead, the consecrated host goes where he would have sat, underlining in visual terms the Catholic belief that the consecrated host is literally Jesus. Even in the vessels of the Mass, the iconography was clear. For example, a chalice commissioned by Pope Paul V at the start of the 17th century (Figure 8) was created with a scene of the Last Supper depicted in the hollowed-out knop.

7. **Monstrance by Johannes Zeckl (Augsburg, 1705).**

8. Chalice commissioned by Pope Paul V (early 17th century).

More widely, the Catholic Reformation instigated a visual revolution, a period of creativity that pushed aside older Renaissance approaches. Baroque was the new style of this Tridentine movement and, like much of the Catholic Reformation, had little or nothing to do with the Council of Trent. Similarly, it was not just confined to the ecclesiastical, but set the tone for secular works as well. An extensive architectural and artistic remodelling programme was required to amend and adapt church architecture to suit the Tridentine liturgy and convey fundamental sacramental teachings. This burst of renewal was given extra impetus by two factors: firstly, the reclamation of lands lost to Protestantism but now in need of re-Catholicization meant new buildings were needed or, at the very least, redecoration to repair what had been damaged; secondly, the new religious orders needed to establish themselves, requiring their own bases and material apparatus. These factors led to the Church becoming a major patron of artistic renewal.

Rome itself was architecturally transformed. Michelangelo's dome of St Peter's Basilica was finished in 1590, followed in the opening decades of the 17th century by the completion of the basilica's façade. Gianlorenzo Bernini, a major figure in the period, then oversaw the full baroque makeover of St Peter's, designing the piazza in front of the basilica and erecting the baldacchino above the altar over the tomb of St Peter. As the 17th century moved into the 18th, 140 statues of saints were added to Bernini's colonnade, from more historically distant figures, such as Thomas Aquinas and Benedict, to the new heroes of the Catholic Reformation, such as Teresa of Avila, Rose of Lima, Francis Xavier, and Francis de Sales. All the statues looked towards St Peter's as the heart of Catholicism, except one, which faced out to the city of Rome and the world; the 12th-century St Norbert had preached devotion to the Real Presence of Christ in the eucharist and here his statue, holding aloft a monstrance, did so again, this time in service of the Catholic Reformation.

Away from St Peter's, major new churches were erected in the city for the new orders, including the Gesú and San Ignazio for the Jesuits, Chiesa Nuova for the Oratorians, and Sant'Andrea della Valle for the Theatines. The Gesù became a model for baroque design, especially after it was reworked in the 17th century, inspiring church architecture from Peru to China. Eschewing the traditional cruciform design, emphasis was instead placed on practicality: the central space was designed as one for preaching and performing the sacraments, with light filling the 'arena'. Charles Borromeo himself had drawn up guidance for reformed church architecture that advised emphasizing the importance of the high altar by raising it up three steps, thus helping to underline that the church was the theatre of salvation. Yet it was not only larger church projects that embraced the baroque movement: the Discalced Carmelite church of Santa Maria della Vittoria was a baroque overload and housed Bernini's famous statue of Teresa of Avila in ecstasy.

After the end of the Thirty Years War, the baroque movement came to dominate the rebuilding process in the Holy Roman Empire. From great Benedictine abbeys, like that at Melk in Austria, to statement churches such as the Karlskirche in Vienna—tellingly dedicated to Charles Borromeo—to secular constructions such as the city's Schönbrunn Palace, baroque took on a different flavour in this region, drifting towards the rococo not just across Austria, but in places like Bavaria and Prague.

Baroque architecture also had its global interpretations, such as at the Jesuit-constructed church of St Peter the Apostle in Andahuaylillas, Peru, or at a number of churches in India. Although some were more western in design than others, cultural accommodation in places like Goa saw Hindu influence in the architecture mingle with the baroque. Often, churches were constructed on sites locals previously believed to be holy, as was done in China and Japan, not only to show that Christianity was the 'triumphant' religion, but also to emphasize it as the conclusion of, or last word on, all that is holy. On occasion, architects even dropped the traditional east–west alignment when building such churches so they could fit into these ancient spaces. Baroque grew to be the expression of Catholic Reformation architecture all over the world and it was adapted accordingly.

The Council of Trent's final session in December 1563 had briefly touched upon art. While stressing its importance as a means of catechesis and rejuvenating personal spirituality, the council delegates insisted that the fantastical and the nude had no place in church art; emphasis instead should be placed on Christian truth and realism. Notoriously, this led to several instances of nudity in Michelangelo's *Last Judgement*, which adorned the altar wall of the Sistine Chapel, being covered up only a couple of decades after its completion.

Realistic, natural, and connected to contemporary life, baroque also defined the Catholic Reformation style of art. These qualities were embodied in the work of the Italian painter Caravaggio, who literally recruited people from the streets to use as models in his artwork. Employing vivid colours and a dynamic use of light, such as in his *The Calling of St Matthew*, Caravaggio also epitomized the baroque taste for the violent, bloody, brutal depiction of martyrdom, such as his *The Incredulity of Saint Thomas*, where the apostle sticks his finger right into Jesus' wound. Similarly, Niccoló Circignani created a fresco cycle in the English College at Rome that emphasized the history of English Catholicism, culminating in brutal depictions of contemporary martyrs from that very institution. A print edition of the images was soon in circulation. The Spanish painter Francisco de Zurbarán also utilized light and dark to paint several otherworldly paintings of St Francis of Assisi, conveying something of the supernatural ecstasy of the saints. One of the most famous examples of this is Bernini's sculpture of Teresa of Avila in which he depicted the angel of divine love piercing her heart, sending her into a religious rapture (Figure 9).

9. Gianlorenzo Bernini, *The Ecstasy of Saint Teresa* (mid-17th century).

As with architecture, baroque art took off in regions that had experienced iconoclasm and were undergoing re-Catholicization. It was similarly localized, whether that be by Georges de La Tour after the French Wars of Religion, or in a major centre like Antwerp following the Protestant iconoclasm of the Dutch Revolt. In the latter, the Jesuit architect Peter Huyssens constructed a baroque church dedicated to Charles Borromeo, its ceilings adorned by 39 paintings by another famed artist of the Catholic Reformation, Peter Paul Rubens. Rubens also painted major altar pieces of Ignatius of Loyola and Francis Xavier for the city's cathedral. None of this was decoration for its own sake; particular messages were conveyed and victories celebrated in the art of the Catholic Reformation. For example, the church of Santa Maria Vittoria was built in Rome in 1621 to commemorate the Catholic victory at the battle of White Mountain, a painting in the interior depicting the Virgin crushing heresy in the form of a serpent. Similarly, Pius V had commissioned paintings to celebrate the victory at the battle of Lepanto that were designed to be hung in the Vatican. Away from confessional competition, the Jesuit Andrea Pozzo's ceiling fresco of the *Glorification of St Ignatius* at San Ignazio in Rome used pioneering techniques to create the impression that the flat ceiling was actually curved, rising upwards towards the fresco's culmination of the founder of the Jesuits being welcomed into heaven by God himself, conveying Jesuit triumph.

Nor was it just high art that went baroque in the Catholic Reformation: a torrent of engravings, woodcuts, and statues shaped popular piety. Devotional prints permeated the homes of the laity as deliberate catechetical and missionary tools. The Spanish Netherlands was again at the forefront, with Antwerp printers producing a stream of affordable devotional prints making Catholic Reformation themes available to the laity in their homes. These prints frequently combined images with some explanatory text or prayers. They were used to teach children the faith, purchased as pilgrimage mementoes, or produced to commemorate certain moments. For example, in 1609 in Brussels, the Jesuits undertook a mass distribution of engravings about Ignatius of Loyola's life to celebrate his beatification. In the 1660s, the Society distributed 30,000 prints of Francis Xavier in Mechelen alone.

As in the medieval period, visual material was deployed to help spread the gospel to the illiterate and the less educated. A particularly striking example was the taolennou of the La Retraite sisters in 17th-century Brittany, who pioneered spiritual retreats for women. The sisters used images for catechesis, underlining the missionary impulse always present in the Catholic Reformation. The visual took on an especially prominent role in the arena of global mission. Recognizing the importance of imagery, albeit in a destructive manner, the earliest Franciscan missionaries destroyed examples of local iconography in modern-day Mexico, deeming it to be pagan, and sought to replace it with Christian symbolism.

As the Catholic Reformation developed, a more collaborative approach began to take hold among the Franciscan and Jesuit missionaries. A Franciscan friar, Jacobo de Testera, used imagery influenced by local art to create documents aimed at evangelizing an area before the local languages were known. These Testerian catechisms came to be used throughout South America in the 17th and 18th centuries. Moreover, the local and universal met in devotional images, such as that of the Virgin of the Rosary of Guápolo created by a Peruvian artist around 1680; it mixed indigenous artistic methods with those more commonly associated with the traditional Iberian approach in order to convey the Virgin's importance.

As previously outlined, the character of the mission in Asia was different from that in South America, and this was evident in its approach to visual culture. Figures in the Gospel stories were depicted with local features and wearing regional clothing. The Jesuits fostered a particular devotion to an icon of the Virgin and child known as the Salus Populi Romani, which was kept in the Roman basilica of Santa Maria Maggiore. It was believed to have been created by St Luke and the Jesuits had it copied throughout their missions, each time adapting it to local customs. Matteo Ricci presented a version to the Chinese emperor.

Similarly, the *Adnotationes et Meditationes in Evangelia* by the Spanish Jesuit Jerónimo Nadal had been published in 1595, and used large pictorial engravings to tell the life of Christ. It quickly became a tool for the global mission. In China, the Jesuit João da Rocha passed the work to Chinese artists as a template, and the images were quickly adapted to fit their environment. For example, the annunciation was shown as taking place in a Chinese-style building, the Virgin and the angel Gabriel depicted as local people wearing traditional clothing (Figure 10).

10. The Annunciation in *Song nian zhu gui cheng* (c.1619).

In other words, the peoples of the different global missionary territories were not passive receivers of art, but helped create and shape the Catholic Reformation in print, sculpture, and architecture. Both sides ensured the merging of Christian iconography with motifs and modes of local cultures. If the aim of Catholic Reformation art was to teach the faith to the masses through the visual, then this is exactly what inculturation and accommodation did, by exporting then adapting the baroque to different surroundings.

Spirituality

The sensory revolution even touched spirituality as it sought to encourage personal, internal reform and commitment. Naturally, traditional forms of spirituality persisted; indeed, mysticism continued to flourish, particularly among female icons of the Catholic Reformation, such as Teresa of Avila and Rose of Lima, as well as the Italian Carmelite nun Maria Magdalena de' Pazzi. It could even be argued that female mystical experience—although regularly a cause of official concern, particularly for the more censorious Iberian Church—blazed the path for famous male mystics, like the Spanish Carmelite friar John of the Cross, who acknowledged the influence of Teresa of Avila.

Equally, the roots of Catholic Reformation spirituality were in the past; it was about developing these traditions, rather than jettisoning and starting again. This understanding is especially evident in the first of the emerging dominant strains of Tridentine spirituality. Ignatius of Loyola's *Spiritual Exercises* were published in 1548, as the blueprint for the Society of Jesus' approach. It was never intended to be read as a book, but rather as a set of guidance notes for those leading a 30-day retreat in what Ignatius termed the spiritual exercises. With medieval roots in mental prayer and methodical meditation, the exercises aimed to settle the retreatant first into a pattern of prayer, then helped them discern God's will for them, before encouraging them to embrace it.

Fundamental to the exercises was the sensory nature of the meditations. Going beyond what was written in the text, the retreat leader—that is, a Jesuit—encouraged the individual to put themselves in the biblical scene. For example, when meditating on the nativity story, the individual was to imagine the road from Nazareth to Bethlehem, its length, the terrain, the surrounding environment, before contemplating the birth scene by hearing the sounds of the cattle, the rustle of the straw; smelling the animals; hearing the sounds of the night. Engaging the senses in this way encouraged the individual to enter into, and to see themselves within, salvation history. The approach was open to anyone. Ignatian spirituality was hugely influential, prompting many clergy to strive to engage and inspire feelings among their congregation during sermons.

Although the Ignatian approach touched on the core Catholic Reformation principle of personal spiritual reform, it was actually another dominant strain of spirituality that really pushed this aspect. Francis de Sales had been a committed evangelist among the Calvinist-leaning peasants of the Chablais region in the duchy of Savoy. He was an associate of Madame Acarie in Paris, who had introduced the Teresian Carmelite reform to France, later entering religious life as Marie de l'Incarnation. This reformist background inspired de Sales's tenure as bishop of Geneva, during which time he exemplified an ideal version of the Tridentine bishop, committed to winning converts by charity and example rather than force. He was a great spiritual guide to many; his role in the founding of the Visitation Order has already been mentioned, but it was his advice to a laywoman about how to live the Christian life that had an even wider impact. The guidance he provided formed the basis of his 1609 publication *Introduction to a Devout Life*. De Sales argued in his text that a person did not have to retreat to a monastic house to live a Christian life, but could do so in the world. He was thus outlining the idea of a lay vocation, guiding people to an exemplary Christian life that would sanctify the world. In his vision, all are called to make a spiritual commitment that leads to sanctity, and it is easy to see how such a model could, for example, inspire Vincent de Paul and his movement in France.

De Sales's work went through at least 40 editions by the time of his death in 1622, and his manifesto helps explain how, for example, in areas where missionary work was illegal, such as Japan and England, the laity could be inspired to play such a vital role in keeping the faith alive. Indeed, the Catholic Reformation increasingly focused on lay spirituality, such as *Perfection in all the States of Christian Life* by the Spanish Jesuit Luis de la Puente, published in 1615. Another good example of popular devotional material is that of the Dominican Luis de Granada, whose work appeared in Japanese translation in 1599, shortly after his death. There were many other spiritual currents within the Catholic Reformation, but it was the Ignatian and Salesian approaches that were dominant.

Aural culture

The Catholic Reformation sought to transform the aural as well as the visual world. In its belt-tightening mode, the Council of Trent worked to ensure due reverence at Mass by banishing 'from the churches all such music which, whether by the organ or in the singing, contains things that are lascivious or impure', in other words, showing off for the sake of virtuosity. Liturgical music had been a focus of criticism of the early Catholic reformers, partly because of its inappropriateness, but more importantly because the words were often not intelligible thanks to overly complex settings. As such, in their estimation, liturgical music was not aiding personal spiritual commitment.

The Tridentine missal, produced in 1570 under Pope Pius V, sought to restore the original purity of the liturgy for the Mass, causing some previous liturgical music to be made redundant. It was replaced by a new style that emphasized clarity of the words, as well as taking on new ideas about duration and technique. The use of polyphony—that is, different voices and/or instruments singing/playing different parts—was streamlined and shortened to aid comprehension. Polyphony was sometimes combined with plainchant, composers on occasion alternating verses between the two. These changes saw, for example, Charles Borromeo commission new liturgical music, which emphasized intelligibility. Despite the Roman curia attempting to limit musical accompaniment to just the organ, feast day liturgies often remained particularly luscious, to the extent that by the mid-17th century, 12 separate choirs sang Vespers at St Peter's Basilica to mark the feast of SS Peter and Paul, with one choir even performing from the walkway in the basilica's dome.

A major figure in shaping this new Tridentine music was Giovanni Pierluigi da Palestrina, who produced a volume of Masses in 1567. He worked on revising plainchant at the behest of Pope Gregory XIII, and was based at St Peter's Basilica in Rome from 1571 until his death in 1594. Italy was a beacon of this new movement and its influence spread internationally, from the Venetian school's impact in northern Europe to the Roman school's effect in Spain and its empire, Tomás Luis de Victoria providing models in the Roman style that would influence composition in the Iberian world.

This musical movement spread globally, Dominicans and Jesuits bringing western musical tradition to, for example, the Philippines, though with frequent cultural accommodation, European and indigenous musical styles existing side by side. As ever within the Catholic Reformation, the influence was not all in one direction; the Portuguese Jesuit Tomás Pereira spent 36 years at the Chinese emperor's court, studying local musical theory and writing Chinese hymns. Vernacular singing and rhyme were used for catechetical purposes in the global arena, while missionaries also made frequent use of *contrafacta*, which was the practice of taking local songs or melodies and replacing the words with catechetical text.

Such non-liturgical music was also harnessed within Catholic Europe, including Philip Neri's Oratorians spreading printed devotional songs known as *lauda* throughout Italy, while singing in confraternity processions was a regular sonic experience for laypeople of both sexes. It is clear that some women possessed musical abilities before entering convents, but it is equally evident that nuns invested in musical training in order to better perform their liturgies, with other instruments supplementing the trained singing of the nuns. These elements demonstrate the Catholic Reformation harnessing music to add to the sensory assault.

The Jesuits strongly encouraged singing in their Marian sodalities, but also deployed it in the dramas performed in their colleges. As with music, drama became a means of instilling Catholic Reformation values. Playwrights from religious orders such as the Franciscans and the Jesuits stressed the connection between an active life in the world and Christian virtues, making their tales both universal and personal, detailing the triumph of believers over adversity. This was made particularly evident in plays about the early Christian Church and its persecution, the link to contemporary events in places on the peripheries of global Catholic reform being obvious; for example, persecuted English Catholics appeared in Jesuit dramas penned for audiences in the Polish–Lithuanian Commonwealth. Similarly, the global missionary arena was the backdrop for performances aimed at European audiences, moral lessons inculcated through plays set in, for example, Japan and India. Biblical themes were equally common and, increasingly in the 17th century, plays that responded to Protestant anti-Catholic dramas. Nonetheless, the principal impetus remained the same: the instillation of Christian morals and encouragement of personal spiritual reform.

The Jesuits were at the forefront of this sacralization of an outwardly secular entertainment, repurposing drama for the Catholic Reformation. Avoiding immorality, drama played a key role in the Society's colleges, helping improve students' oratorial skills and proficiency in Latin, but also heading out of the confines of the building and into the vernacular to be performed in the public arena as significant social events. These plays might last for days with a cast of hundreds, as they did in Munich. Given such a context, it is not surprising that several leading dramatists of the 17th century were schooled at Jesuit colleges, including the French playwright Molière, and Calderón, who gave impetus to a golden age of Spanish theatre.

Nevertheless, the important point remains that theatre was harnessed as yet another missionary tool. In South America, Franciscans tapped into indigenous traditions to work with local converts to write plays in the vernacular. They adapted plays written in Europe for a new audience, tweaking them to appeal to the different culture, such as increasing the role of the Virgin Mary to chime with Indian devotion to her. It should not, therefore, be surprising that a figure like Matthias Sámbár, one of the most famous Jesuit missionaries in the re-Catholicization of Hungary during the 17th century, was also a playwright.

Intellectual culture

The Catholic Reformation was all encompassing, touching every facet of life experience, and intellectual culture was no exception. Each of the preceding chapters has underlined the importance of education within the Catholic Reformation, whether that be training a better clergy through the creation of seminaries, increased educational opportunities for the laity, or the establishment of dedicated teaching orders such as the Piarists and the De La Salle Brothers. The education of girls was not neglected, with traditional contemplative orders running schools for that purpose, and orders such as the Ursulines prioritizing female educational provision.

Although the Index existed, the Catholic Reformation was certainly not anti-book. In fact, the existence of the Index can be seen as a tacit acknowledgement that the Catholic Reformation recognized the power of reading and so sought to harness it. Books were published in a range of languages; not only dictionaries by missionaries in languages such as Vietnamese, Thai, Armenian, and Angolese, but also devotional books for that global market. Indeed, although the Tridentine liturgy was uniform and set in Latin, a Chinese-language liturgy was authorized for much of the 17th century, meaning a translation was even made of the Roman missal.

Vernacular bibles, despite being frowned upon by the Index, were produced and came to be accepted in the more confessionally contested areas of northern Europe, including Germany, Switzerland, and Bohemia. A well-known production was the English-language translation of the New Testament published in 1582, with the Old Testament following nearly 30 years later. Principally the work of Gregory Martin at the missionary English College at Douai, it included authoritative commentary on the text to counter Protestant interpretations. It became the inspiration for a similar undertaking in the Polish–Lithuanian Commonwealth, underlining the use of local language in global missionary territories closer to the traditional heartlands of Catholic Europe. Equally, language could be harnessed as a means of inculcating Tridentine identity, such as the use of the Irish language by Franciscans to create a positive correlation between Catholicism and national identity.

The most significant genre of production in the Catholic Reformation was religious books in local languages, though China was a little different. Missionaries sought to win Chinese converts through showing the advanced nature of western, so implicitly Christian, science and classical learning. Strictly religious books were still the majority, but works of secular learning were thus also harnessed in the Chinese missionary field. This highlights the breadth of Catholic books produced more generally, covering physics, mathematics, philosophy, history, and a variety of literary works. Geography showed the reciprocal relationship between centres and peripheries in the Catholic Reformation, accounts of voyages and descriptive texts of places such as Japan, China, India, and Ethiopia being produced. Local converts such as Xu Guangqi and Yang Tingyuan also produced works defending Catholicism in China.

All this reinforces that the intellectual culture of the Catholic Reformation was diverse, with there being no one set Catholic approach to method or expectation. Philosophical and scientific developments could be constrained by the Church (infamously in the case of Galileo), though not always. For example, the Frenchman Marin Mersenne, a member of the Minims, a Franciscan reform movement from the 15th century, corresponded with Thomas Hobbes and René Descartes. Other examples are plentiful, suggesting that even if people limited their speculative work in the wake of the Galileo affair, the Catholic Reformation nevertheless produced a number of significant intellectual interventions. For example, the German Jesuit Christopher Clavius, a mathematician and astronomer, was instrumental in introducing the Gregorian calendar reforms in 1582, which changed the dating system of most of Europe. The Spanish Jesuit Francisco Suárez was arguably the most influential voice in law and philosophy, the German Jesuit Athanasius Kircher a renowned polymath, while the Italian Jesuit Robert Bellarmine theorized extensively on the pope's rights in temporal affairs, the question of authority in the secular and spiritual spheres of life a pressing concern of the early modern period.

It is also worth recognizing a project aimed at producing a scholarly account of the lives of the saints, trimmed of the legends and accretions found in the medieval *Golden Legend*. Its real architect was the Flemish Jesuit Jean Bolland, and his team from the 1630s, whose *Acta Sanctorum* started to appear in the 1640s, provided the Church with a calendar of the saints. They became known as the Bollandists and the huge undertaking is still ongoing, despite attracting the interest of the Spanish Inquisition in the late 17th century. These examples do reveal a danger, however, as while the influence of the Jesuits was significant, there is a risk that they receive too much focus, partly because of availability of sources, but also due to the order prioritizing academic endeavour and the promotion of scholarly work about itself. This means other influential religious orders have been neglected. For example, a branch of Benedictines, the Maurists, established in France in 1621, were known for their scholarship, including that of the historian Jean Mabillon. By the 18th century, exile Scottish Benedictines were significant figures in the Bavarian Academy of Science and educational provision in the whole region. The Italian Oratorian Caesar Baronius wrote on the history of the Church, the first volume of his *Ecclesiastical Annals* appearing in 1588.

Intellectual culture also included laypeople such as the French philosopher Blaise Pascal, while more research is needed into female contributions, such as the books produced by a huge number of women religious, for both internal and external audiences. All of these intellectual efforts were undertaken not as ends in themselves, but for the glory of God. Admittedly, in several fields, Catholic Reformation figures were meeting Protestant challenges head on, the study of history itself having become a battlefield. Yet, overall, the Catholic Reformation touched everything, not only encompassing but actively harnessing the senses and the intellect in its reshaping—and reforming—of the world.

Chapter 7
Legacies

In 1942, George Orwell, whose works include *Animal Farm* and *Nineteen Eighty-Four*, wrote: 'It would be putting it too crudely to say that every poet in our time must either die young, enter the Catholic Church, or join the Communist Party, but in fact the escape from the consciousness of futility is along these general lines.' Orwell was giving voice to the prevalent feeling of his time about the need for change and the improvement of the human condition. While doing so, he was not arguing that people should convert to Catholicism—far from it in fact—but was recognizing that it was a serious idea, which sought to reform the world and, just as importantly, promoted a coherent, joined-up vision that incorporated all facets of life. This all-encompassing element was central to the Catholic Reformation, including both the expected—such as spirituality and theology—and the less predictable, like architecture and history-writing. Medieval conceptions of Christianity ranged widely, but it was the spirit of Tridentine Catholicism that championed total reform.

That term Tridentine Catholicism has been used deliberately, as the term post-Tridentine for the Catholicism that came after the Council of Trent takes a very narrow view of the Catholic Reformation. Certainly, it is one that makes little sense liturgically. Remarkably, Pius V's Roman missal of 1570 remained the norm, with minor tweaks, in the Latin rite of the Catholic Church until

Pope Paul VI's revision in 1969. In other words, for 400 years the Tridentine rite was the standard form of the Mass. Equally, if the Catholic Reformation is tied too closely to the Council of Trent, then explaining what was happening in areas on the peripheries of Catholic reform—particularly contested areas of persecution, where the decrees of the council were not officially promulgated till centuries after it closed—becomes even more challenging.

Controversies over approach

None of that should imply that the path of Catholic reform was smooth, and liturgy is a case in point. After the success of accommodation and inculturation in the 17th century, the global missionary effort subsequently became mired in several contentions. The most famous example was the Chinese Rites controversy. Following Matteo Ricci's lead, Jesuit missionaries in China had amalgamated certain Chinese customs and Confucianism with Catholic practice and beliefs. By the 1630s, Spanish Dominicans had started to arrive in the country from the Philippines, soon to be joined by Franciscans and Augustinians. Typical of the Spanish outlook, these missionaries rejected accommodation and took aim at three particular aspects of the approach: the reverence due to Confucius as part of Chinese social life; the practice of ancestor worship, which involved ceremonies at the graves of the deceased; and terminology, as the Jesuits sought to find the correct wording in places like China where there was no equivalent 'God' concept in the vocabulary.

In the first two instances, Ricci and the Jesuits had decided that these were part of the culture of Chinese society, and not religious in character. Equally, ancestor worship ceremonies could be tweaked to align with practices around praying for the souls in purgatory. It is therefore not difficult to see how such accommodationist approaches clashed with an Iberian missionary mindset that prioritized Europeanization. As for the language issue, this was also a problem in different global missionary arenas, and Ricci had settled for a term that roughly translated as 'Lord of Heaven'.

Even within the Jesuit order, Ricci's approach was contentious and after his death tensions grew as other concessions were granted to the Chinese mission, including permission to celebrate the liturgy in Chinese as opposed to Latin, and to wear Chinese-style headpieces during the celebration of Mass. After a major flare-up around these matters in the middle of the 17th century, further oil was poured on the fire by the arrival of French missionaries. In order to disrupt Iberian dominance, the papacy increasingly turned to French clergy from the Paris Foreign Missions Society to fill episcopal vacancies in the global missionary arena. In 1687, Charles Maigrot was appointed vicar apostolic of Fukion. Five years later, the Chinese emperor issued an edict of toleration officially allowing Chinese citizens to embrace Catholicism. The following year, with spectacularly poor judgement, Maigrot banned Chinese Catholics from honouring Confucius and attending ancestor worship ceremonies.

Battle lines were quickly drawn between the advocates of the different missionary positions, with the Jesuits only further escalating the situation by requesting the emperor intervene with the pope on the issue. By 1706 de-escalation was impossible after papal condemnation of ancestor worship. Maigrot was expelled from China and the emperor insisted that all European missionaries must swear to follow 'the way of Father Ricci' if they were to remain in the kingdom. In 1715, Clement XI condemned the Ricci approach that had brought such rewards, a position reaffirmed by Benedict XIV in 1745. Sporadic persecution of Catholics increased into the 19th century as European missionaries were expelled and banned from entering the country, with Chinese clergy stepping into the void. At around the same time, accommodationist principles were also condemned in India, where French Capuchins were particularly critical of Jesuit assimilation methods in what came to be known as the Malibar Rites Controversy. These clashes were a legacy of the tension between uniformity and diversity in the Catholic Reformation.

Missionary approach within the Catholic Reformation was not the only cause of future fissures: theological innovations could lead to claims of heresy. A possible way of understanding these different interpretations is to view them as rejected paths down which the Catholic Reformation could have ventured. For most of the period after the Council of Trent, until they were silenced by the pope in 1607, Dominicans and Jesuits sparred over the role of God's grace and man's free will in his salvation, a topic that had much occupied Protestant reformers. This debate took particular hold in France and grew during the 17th and 18th centuries into the Jansenism controversy.

Taking its name from one of its early proponents, Cornelius Jansen, Jansenism put into overdrive the Augustinian belief in the sinfulness of man and the world. Theologically pessimistic, it emphasized the huge impact of original sin on human nature, downplaying—and even questioning—the role of human activity and free will in the work of salvation. Jansenists took special aim at what they considered a creeping laxity in Tridentine Catholicism, particularly embodied by the Jesuit approach to confession and absolution that focused too much on judging the act, as opposed to the role of moral attitudes or better behaviour in salvation. For them, corrupt human nature meant only a very few would reach heaven. The Jesuits retorted that the new situations of a rapidly changed world required a flexible approach. A pamphlet war raged and the topic became a pressing one, particularly in France, with the philosopher Blaise Pascal involved as a Jansenist sympathizer. Indeed, his sister Jacqueline was a nun at the Jansenist stronghold of Port-Royal. Jansenist views were effectively prohibited by Clement XI's papal bull *Unigenitus* (1713), though its ramifications rumbled on in France.

Several key Catholic Reformation themes are evident within the Jansenist controversy. Unsurprisingly, the Jansenists opposed the Jesuits in the Chinese Rites controversy, seeing no virtue in ancestor worship as it was not explicitly Christian. This reveals something wider: the Jansenists were fundamentally against Jesuit principles of accommodation, not just in the global mission, but in terms of accommodation to the modern world. A crude division can be drawn between Jansenists advocating a theology frozen in aspic since the church fathers, and Jesuits striving to interpret Catholicism for the changing times. Naturally, the Jansenist response was always to ask where such accommodation would eventually lead, but the characterization can mask something important. Like the Jesuits, many Jansenists believed in frequent confession and communion, hallmarks of the Catholic Reformation. In short, the Jansenists represented another interpretation of how to undertake Catholic reform, albeit one that, officially, in the end, turned to error.

Moreover, as elsewhere in the Catholic Reformation, contrasting interpretations fell roughly along existing contours of religious life, this time largely between secular clergy and the Jesuits. It is not surprising that the debate really took hold in France, where voices were frequently raised in support of episcopal authority—that is, the right of a bishop within his diocese—against perceived papal repression, such as that against Jansenism. The role of the bishop was a major question never really settled by the Catholic Reformation, and one that was particularly pointed in the French Gallican Church system. Nevertheless, at the root of the Jansenism controversy was that perennial theme at the heart of the Catholic Reformation: the role of the Catholic in the world. Indeed, its centrality is equally evident in another theological dead end eventually condemned as heresy. In the late 17th century, particularly in France, quietism raised the status of contemplation over all other endeavours, to the point of mental inactivity and self-annihilation in order to let God work on the individual as a blank slate. This was clearly a very different understanding of the Catholic Reformation from that embodied by Salesian spirituality and the activities of a figure like Vincent de Paul.

Such theological battles did not, of course, happen in a void. For example, the Jansenist controversy had significant political repercussions in France. With its downplaying of free will, Jansenism made God seem arbitrary in his actions or lack of them, creating a fatalistic attitude to faith that became the target of Voltaire's Enlightenment polemic. At the same time, France and other countries increasingly pushed back against perceived Jesuit papalism, ultimately resulting in the order's suppression by Pope Clement XIV in 1773. All this helped lead to the French Revolution, the event frequently seen as the dividing line between the early modern and the modern period.

Perpetual reform

To adopt this chronological divide is to limit the legacy of the Catholic Reformation. Catholic reform was not confined to a few decades after the Council of Trent, but continued to inspire new initiatives, whether that be the Trappists' austere reform of lax Cistercian life in the second half of the 17th century, or Alphonsus Liguori's Redemptorists and their dedication to parochial missions in 18th-century Italy. Rather than being staid, Tridentine Catholicism was powered by this reform impulse, which existed before the Council of Trent, but was fully unleashed in the Catholic Reformation. One area of much recent historical interest has been around the idea of a Catholic Enlightenment. Some proponents of the Catholic Enlightenment clearly interpreted their intellectual endeavours as the best means of achieving true spiritual reform. In other words, it was another way of interpreting and seeking the best means to bring about the Catholic Reformation.

The French Revolution did not end that impulse; in fact, it revived questions and ideas that had dominated the Catholic

Reformation. The participants at the Council of Trent had never explicitly touched on the role of the papacy and its relationship to bishops. It remained a thorny issue, as evidenced in the Jansenist controversy. Atheistic French revolutionaries ushered in fierce repression of the Church, yet a new movement rose from the smouldering wreck of the Catholic Enlightenment and what could be termed more accommodationist attitudes. Its advocates believed such approaches represented a wrong turn that could only have resulted in tragedy, presenting as evidence the execution of Catholics in France, the expulsion of religious orders, and the Church's decreased role in public life. In response, a number of Catholics advocated a dominant ultramontanism; that is, a belief in papal primacy, placing great power in the pope in order to ensure discipline and unity within the Church as it faced an increasingly hostile world. Its high point was the church council Vatican I, which in 1870 pronounced papal infallibility as dogma. This did not mean that the pope could never do wrong, but rather declared that, when speaking as the successor of St Peter on matters of faith, he could not err and had the final say. In reality, this claim has been rarely enforced, but, more importantly, it shows that questions around the relationship between the pope and bishops remained a live issue. The strongest ultramontane popes, Pius IX and Pius X, fell back on tools of the Catholic Reformation period, namely the Index and the Inquisition, though giving them greater prominence than previously. Ultramontanism also introduced an oath against modernism, that is the rejection of employing modern techniques in interpreting scripture and adapting it to the contemporary world. Again, it is not difficult to see early modern debates about mission strategy and accommodation being played out here. Another Catholic Reformation strand reached fruition in 1854, when Pope Pius IX pronounced the Immaculate Conception of Mary as dogma, a theological issue debated since medieval times but, as we have seen, given major impetus by the Franciscans during the Catholic Reformation.

Other 19th-century legacies of the Catholic Reformation away from high church politics were evident, whether that be parish missions or the importance of female devotional practices. In those countries where Catholicism had been prohibited for centuries, such as England, Catholics went about attempting to implement the decrees of the Council of Trent, such as establishing diocesan seminaries. Despite the rules of enclosure issued by the Council of Trent, there had been a steady rise from the late 17th century in unenclosed, active communities of women religious. The number exploded in the 19th century as new congregations pioneered female education and different forms of social activism, their roots firmly planted in the spirit of the Catholic Reformation. In Europe at least, the 19th century witnessed a religious revival across the Christian Churches and the Catholic Church was no exception. In that sense, it echoed the Catholic Reformation's mission to reform the individual's soul and encourage witness to their faith in the world. These ongoing connections were given physical expression when Catholic missionaries were again permitted to enter Japan in the late 19th century. Almost two centuries had passed since the expulsion of the last priest, but the modern missionaries discovered a living and breathing legacy of the Catholic Reformation: an underground community of laypeople who still identified themselves as Christians.

A case could even be made that the 19th century did not mark the end of the Catholic Reformation's legacies. The Second Vatican Council of 1962 to 1965 can be understood to have swept away much of the Tridentine Church. However, it could be argued that it was still dealing with the same tensions stored up by the Catholic Reformation. Certainly, it looked to rebalance, once again, the relationship between bishops and the papacy, a negotiation still ongoing today with Pope Francis's push towards synodality. Catholic Reformation figures provided inspiration for new 20th-century pioneers, such as Anjezë Gonxhe Bojaxhiu, better known as Mother Teresa of Calcutta, who was encouraged in her work by the example of Mary Ward and her unenclosed

'Jesuitesses'. Dynamism and adaptation returned to the fore, whether that be depictions of Our Lady of China or local liturgical customs in churches in Africa. On a different trajectory, pilgrimage to sites connected to the miraculous remains a mainstay of modern Catholicism, such as the popularity of Lourdes in France. Similarly, the cult of martyrdom remains strong, from the likes of Oscar Romero, murdered by the oppressive regime in El Salvador, to the martyrs of Communism, such as Jerzy Popiełuszko in Poland. All these phenomena have their roots in the Catholic Reformation; accommodationist missionary activity did not end, while engaging with the secular, whether in partnership or opposition, remained a delicate and controversial matter.

All this leads towards a sense of never-ending reform within Catholicism. Nevertheless, what is evident is that arbitrary time boundaries are blurred and breached where the Catholic Reformation is concerned. At the core of the Catholic Reformation was personal commitment to God, reforming both the individual and the Church in order to achieve it. That understanding of reform was a real legacy unleashed by the Catholic Reformation. Paradoxically, it led to its being swept away by Vatican II as the 20th-century council sought to bring that message to the modern world, just as a number of Catholic reformers had sought to do in the early modern period. Ecclesiastically, what was Vatican II if not an attempt to re-energize the faith(ful) for a rapidly changing world, and to inspire inner conviction rather than settle for going through the motions out of habit? That same goal lay at the heart of the Tridentine reforms of the Catholic Reformation.

Owing to the growing number of different Protestant denominations following the Reformation, it is easy to focus more on the fierce debates Protestant reformers had around religion. Those debates also took place in early modern Catholicism, though the participants remained in communion with the papacy, no matter how strained that relationship at times may have become. Ultimately, the Catholic Reformation was a movement encompassing a variety of ideas and approaches. There were different ways of implementing Catholic reform; these were not always competing, and could even sometimes be complementary. In that variety were sown the seeds of its survival and why its legacies can still be seen today.

Further reading

General

Bamji, Alexandra, Geert H. Janssen, and Mary Laven (eds), *The Ashgate Research Companion to the Counter-Reformation* (Farnham, 2013).

Bedouelle, Guy, *The Reform of Catholicism, 1480–1620*, trans. James K. Farge (Toronto, 2008).

Bireley, Robert, *The Refashioning of Catholicism, 1450–1700: A Reassessment of the Counter-Reformation* (Basingstoke, 1999).

Bossy, John, *Christianity in the West, 1400–1700* (Oxford, 1985).

Ditchfield, Simon, 'Catholic Reformation and Renewal', in Peter Marshall (ed.), *The Oxford Illustrated History of the Reformation* (Oxford, 2015), pp. 177–210.

Evennett, H. Outram, *The Spirit of the Counter-Reformation*, ed. John Bossy (Cambridge, 1968).

Hsia, R. Po-Chia, *The World of Catholic Renewal, 1540–1770*, 2nd edn. (Cambridge, 2005).

Iserloh, Erwin, Joseph Glazik, and Hubert Jedin, *History of the Church: Volume 5, Reformation and Counter Reformation*, trans. Anselm Biggs and Peter W. Becker (London, 1980).

Mullett, Michael, *The Catholic Reformation* (London, 1999).

Wright, Anthony D., *The Counter-Reformation: Catholic Europe and the Non-Christian World* (London, 1982).

Chapter 2: The Council of Trent and new soldiers for Christ

Evangelisti, Silvia, *Nuns: A History of Convent Life, 1450–1700* (Oxford, 2008).

François, Wim, and Violet Soen (eds), *The Council of Trent: Reform and Controversy in Europe and beyond (1545–1700)* (Göttingen, 2018).

Headley, John M., and John B. Tomaro (eds), *San Carlo Borromeo: Catholic Reform and Ecclesiastical Politics in the Second Half of the Sixteenth Century* (Washington, 1988).

O'Malley, John W., *Trent and All That: Renaming Catholicism in the Early Modern Era* (Cambridge, Mass., 2000).

O'Malley, John W., *Trent: What Happened at the Council* (Cambridge, Mass., 2013).

Chapter 3: Catholic Europe?

Diefendorf, Barbara B., *Planting the Cross: Catholic Reform and Renewal in Sixteenth- and Seventeenth-Century France* (Oxford, 2019).

Forrestal, Alison, *Vincent de Paul, the Lazarist Mission, and French Catholic Reform* (Oxford, 2017).

Lehfeldt, Elizabeth A., *Religious Women in Golden Age Spain: The Permeable Cloister* (Aldershot, 2005).

Ó hAnnracháin, Tadhg, *Catholic Europe, 1592–1648: Centre and Peripheries* (Oxford, 2015).

Chapter 4: Missionaries and martyrs

Brockey, Liam Matthew, *Journey to the East: The Jesuit Mission to China, 1579–1724* (Cambridge, Mass., 2007).

Chambers, Liam, and Thomas O'Connor (eds), *College Communities in Exile: Education, Migration and Catholicism in Early Modern Europe* (Manchester, 2017).

Ditchfield, Simon, 'Decentering the Catholic Reformation: Papacy and Peoples in the Early Modern World', *Archiv für Reformationsgeschichte*, 101 (2010), pp. 186–208.

Gregory, Brad S., *Salvation at Stake: Christian Martyrdom in Early Modern Europe* (Cambridge, Mass., 1999).

Hsia, R. Po-Chia, *A Jesuit in the Forbidden City: Matteo Ricci, 1552–1610* (Oxford, 2010).

Kaplan, Benjamin J., Bob Moore, Henk van Nierop, and Judith Pollmann (eds), *Catholic Communities in Protestant States: Britain and the Netherlands c.1570–1720* (Manchester, 2009).

Chapter 5: Catholic living

Fosi, Irene, *Inquisition, Conversion, and Foreigners in Baroque Rome* (Leiden, 2020).

Gray, Richard, 'The Papacy and the Atlantic Slave Trade: Lourenco da Silva, the Capuchins and the Decisions of the Holy Office', *Past & Present*, 115 (1987), pp. 52–68.

Lehner, Ulrich L. (ed.), *Innovation in Early Modern Catholic Theology* (London, 2022).

Rapley, Elizabeth, *The Dévotes: Women and Church in Seventeenth-Century France* (Montreal, 1990).

Zupanov, Ines G., and Pierre Antoine Fabre (eds), *The Rites Controversies in the Early Modern World* (Leiden, 2018).

Chapter 6: Sensing and thinking Catholicism

Ivanic, Suzanna, *Catholica: The Visual Culture of Catholicism* (London, 2022).

Lang, Uwe Michael, *The Roman Mass: From Early Christian Origins to Tridentine Reform* (Cambridge, 2022).

Lehner, Ulrich L., *The Inner Life of Catholic Reform: From the Council of Trent to the Enlightenment* (Oxford, 2022).

Tutino, Stefania, *Empire of Souls: Robert Bellarmine and the Christian Commonwealth* (Oxford, 2010).

Zupanov, Ines G. (ed.), *The Oxford Handbook of the Jesuits* (Oxford, 2019).

Index

For the benefit of digital users, indexed terms that span two pages (e.g., 52–53) may, on occasion, appear on only one of those pages.

CATHOLICISM
A Very Short Introduction
Gerald O'Collins

Despite a long history of external threats and internal strife, the Roman Catholic Church and the broader reality of Catholicism remain a vast and valuable presence into the third millennium of world history. What are the origins of the Catholic Church? How has Catholicism changed and adapted to such vast and diverse cultural influences over the centuries? What great challenges does the Catholic Church now face in the twenty-first century, both within its own life and in its relation to others around the world? In this Very Short Introduction, Gerald O'Collins draws on the best current scholarship available to answer these questions and to present, in clear and accessible language, a fresh introduction to the largest and oldest institution in the world.

www.oup.com/vsi

CHRISTIAN ETHICS
A Very Short Introduction
D. Stephen Long

This *Very Short Introduction* to Christian ethics introduces the
topic by examining its sources and historical basis. D. Stephen
Long presents a discussion of the relationship between Christian
ethics, modern, and postmodern ethics, and explores practical
issues including sex, money, and power. Long recognises the
inherent difficulties in bringing together 'Christian' and 'ethics' but
argues that this is an important task for both the Christian faith
and for ethics. Arguing that Christian ethics are not a precise
science, but the cultivation of practical wisdom from a range of
sources, Long also discusses some of the failures of the Christian
tradition, including the crusades, the conquest, slavery,
inquisitions, and the Galileo affair.

www.oup.com/vsi

THE APOCRYPHAL GOSPELS
A Very Short Introduction
Paul Foster

This *Very Short Introduction* offers a clear, accessible, and concise account of the apocryphal gospels - exploring their origins, their discovery, and discussing how the various texts have been interpreted both by the Church and beyond. Paul Foster shows how the apocryphal gospels reflect the diversity that existed within early Christianity, and examines the extent to which they can be used to reconstruct an accurate portrait of the historical Jesus. Including discussions of controversies and case-studies such as the alleged hoax surrounding the discovery of Secret Mark, Foster concludes that the non-canonical texts, considered in the correct context, offer us an important window on the vibrant and multi-faceted face of early Christianity.

> 'He writes with elegance and clarity, and presents...complex arguments...with simplicity and grace.'

Baptist Times

www.oup.com/vsi

THE NEW TESTAMENT
A Very Short Introduction
Luke Timothy Johnson

As part of the Christian Bible, the New Testament is at once widely influential and increasingly unknown. Those who want to know the basics can find in this introduction the sort of information that locates these ancient writings in their historical and literary context. In addition to providing the broad conceptual and factual framework for the New Testament — including the process by which distinct compositions became a sacred book — this introduction provides as well a more detailed examination of specific compositions that have had particularly strong influence, including Paul's letters to the Corinthians and Romans, the four Gospels, and the Book of Revelation.

www.oup.com/vsi

THE BOOKS OF MORMON
A Very Short Introduction
Terryl L. Givens

Terryl Givens provides a concise introduction to the Book of Mormon, outlining not only its controversial origins, but its plot-lines and major themes, its doctrines, its role in the life of the church, and the current state of Book of Mormon scholarship. Written from an insider's perspective, but without advocacy, this book will be the essential guide to this important text. With over 140 million copies in print, and serving as the principal proselytizing tool of one of the world's fastest growing faiths, the Book of Mormon is undoubtedly one of the most influential religious texts produced in the western world.

www.oup.com/vsi

THE QUAKERS
A Very Short Introduction
Pink Dandelion

The Quakers are a fascinating religious group both in their
origins and in the variety of reinterpretations of the faith since.
Emerging from the social unrest of the English civil war, the
Quakers have gone on to have an influence way beyond their
numbers: be it their continued stance against war or their
pioneering work against slavery. At the same time, Quakers
maintain a distinctive worship method to achieve the direct
encounter with God which has been at the heart of the movement
since its beginning. This book charts the history of Quakerism
and its present-day diversity, and outlines its approach to
worship, belief, theology and language, and ecumenism.

www.oup.com/vsi

HUMANISM
A Very Short Introduction
Stephen Law

Religion is currently gaining a much higher profile. The number of faith schools is increasingly, and religious points of view are being aired more frequently in the media. As religion's profile rises, those who reject religion, including humanists, often find themselves misunderstood, and occasionally misrepresented. Stephen Law explores how humanism uses science and reason to make sense of the world, looking at how it encourages individual moral responsibility and shows that life can have meaning without religion. Challenging some of the common misconceptions, he seeks to dispute the claims that atheism and humanism are 'faith positions' and that without God there can be no morality and our lives are left without purpose.

www.oup.com/vsi

CALVINISM
A Very Short Introduction
Jon Balserak

To Calvin, the only thing that mattered was correcting God's church, and his ideas started the movement now known as Calvinism. From Calvin's time, the movement has grown and spread throughout Europe and into North and South America, Africa, and Asia.

In this *Very Short Introduction*, Jon Balserak explores Calvin's life and considers the major ideas associated with the Calvinist system of thought, by which much of contemporary thought has been influenced. Through his informed account, Balserak combats common misconceptions about Calvinism, and explores the relationship between this religion and the modern world.

2
0
4